How Professors Play The Cat Guarding The Cream

Why We're Paying More And Getting Less in Higher Education

Richard M. Huber

GEORGE MASON UNIVERSITY PRESS
Fairfax, Virginia

Copyright © 1992 by
George Mason University Press
4400 University Drive
Fairfax, VA 22030

Distributed by
National Book Network

4720 Boston Way
Lanham, MD 20706

3 Henrietta Street
London WC2E 8LU England

Library of Congress Cataloging-in-Publication Data
Huber, Richard M.
How professors play the cat guarding the cream : why we're paying
more and getting less in higher education / Richard M. Huber.
p.   cm.
Includes bibliographical references and index.
1. Universities and colleges—United States.   2. College costs—
United States.   3. Corporate culture—United States.
4. College teachers—Salaries, etc.—United States.   5. College
students—United States.   6. Universities and colleges—United
States—Administration.   I. Title.
LA227.4.H83   1992   378.73—dc20   92–6338 CIP

ISBN 0–913969–43–5 (cloth : alk. paper)

This Book is for
CINTRA VI, GILLAN,
and for
Their Cousins in the Future

CONTENTS

INTRODUCTION

Michael Lewis was looking for a job. The interview appointment was breakfast at 6:30 a.m. Lewis tells the story in his bestselling *Liar's Poker*, a shrewd memoir about the investment banking firm of Salomon Brothers.

The breakfast interview was with Leo Corbett, the head of Salomon recruiting from New York. "I went through the painful and unnatural process," Lewis recalls, "of rising at 5:30 a.m. and putting on a blue suit to have a business breakfast. But Corbett didn't offer me a job either, just a plate of wet scrambled eggs. We had a pleasant talk, which was disconcerting, because Salomon Brothers' recruiters were meant to be bastards. It seemed clear Corbett wanted me to work at Salomon, but he never came right out and proposed. I went home, took off the suit, and went back to bed."

A puzzled Michael Lewis asked a fellow student what he should do: "Salomon Brothers, he said, never made job offers. It was too smart to give people the chance to turn it down. Salomon Brothers only gave hints. If I had been given a hint that it wanted to hire me, the best thing for me to do was call Leo Corbett in New York and *take* the job from him. So I did. I called him, reintroduced myself, and said, 'I want to let you know that I accept.' 'Glad to have you on board,' he said, and laughed."

To get the job—and get ahead—you have to know the corporate culture. In *most* cases, the swaggering call to Corbett would have been rebuffed with: "Don't call us, we'll call you." In *this* case, the corporate culture of Salomon Brothers responded to an assertive style and Lewis got the job.

The culture of a corporation, like a nation, is a cluster of beliefs that mandate behavior. Business executives are soaked in the conventions of the corporate culture—as well as the nuances of their own company. Just so a university. Faculty, deans, and presidents begin to absorb academic values in graduate school and become needle-point sensitive to the styles of the particular campus that employs them.

1

University culture is a wondrous association of purposes, processes, and people totally unlike business and most non-profit organizations. Universities are unique. That puts most of us at a disadvantage. How can we begin to understand the culture of a university? Comparison is a useful device. Most Americans have a general understanding of how a business operates. After all, "the business of America is business." Comparing a corporation to a university contrasts the familiar with the less familiar for a deeper understanding of both. With comparative insights, parents, students, business executives as trustees, alumni, legislators, and taxpayers can begin to master how universities work. It is for them that this book has been written.

Parents, groaning under the burden of tuition payments, want to know why the bill keeps increasing faster than the rate of inflation. Students, particularly those accepted by the more prestigious campuses, wonder where all the distinguished professors are hiding. Business executives, straining to increase employee productivity in their enterprises, are perplexed about how faculty output is measured. Alumni, contributing with filial devotion to their alma mater, sometimes suspect that the honor of being selected as a member of the board of trustees is not matched by the board's demands for exacting accountability. Citizens, dutifully paying state taxes, are beginning to ask whether they are getting their money's worth on local campuses.

At least two issues emerge from these concerns. The first is to *improve the quality of the product*, in this case a service: The *most serious defect is undergraduate teaching*. The second is the *reduction of costs*: The defect is in productivity. Both concerns may be found and resolved in the performance of the faculty.

University culture is filled with ironies. While irony enriches creative literature, it enfeebles an operating enterprise. Novels show us how irony snarls life with contradictions—we say one thing and mean another, appearance fails to correspond with reality, results do not correspond to expectations. Humor added to irony makes us laugh at life's absurdities. Humor shows up the incongruities. We have found some humor in university culture, but it has not been easy when the contradictions increase tuition charges, decrease teaching effectiveness, and cripple productivity.

Some ironies that emerge from this study follow. The ones listed here, and others in Appendix A, are set down for the moment without the nuances which in later chapters soften their edges:

- The market value of a degree is increased, not by an improvement in the education of undergraduates, but by the faculty's enhanced reputation for scholarship.
- The academic value of a credit earned by an undergraduate is the same whether taught by a full professor or a graduate student. It's also the same price.
- A student at a private university can pay ten times more per course taught by a graduate student than a student at a community college pays while studying under a professor with a doctorate.
- An increasing endowment does not reduce tuition but inflates it.
- A major benefit of attending a private, high-priced university, compared to a cheaper public school, is social class identification.
- The more expensive the tuition, the more likely a campus concern for America's "oppressed victims."
- Preferential treatment for blacks, Hispanics, and Native-Americans accentuates racial/ethnic identification in order to diminish racial/ethnic discrimination.
- Federal and state governments complain about the increase in administrators while passing legislation that requires the services of administrators.
- While the published research of scholars is rigorously evaluated for reliability, the undergraduate teaching of professors is seldom evaluated for the purposes of improvement.
- Universities, specialists in education, do little to educate their educators to be effective teachers.
- Like art made popular by the public, a professor applauded by students raises suspicion in the faculty club of intellectual shallowness.
- In the past half century the teaching hours of faculty in research institutions have been cut in half and the school year reduced by one month while teaching performance, magnified by teaching assistants, has suffered a decline in possibly equal proportions.

How these and other ironies play themselves out in university culture, and the consequences for those touched by their influence, is the story we have to tell.

* * *

The aspiration of this book is to help those involved with a university to ask probing questions of administrators and faculty. The queries lead to a number of doable reforms. The reforms are likely to induce protective inaction. So, tactful questions are often more effective in persuading

3

administrators and faculty to begin to think about the unthinkable—*how does the faculty spend its time.*

Understanding university culture is mandatory for asking the right questions. Together we take a brisk walk through the groves of academe, identifying there the structures and functions that are indispensable for getting a perspective on this major institution in American society.

We can no longer afford to misrepresent the university with the seducer's forgiving eye. This particular gallant complimented a lady who knew her nose to be too large and her lips too thin. "Your face," he cooed to her yielding delight, "is a perfect combination of imperfections." Universities are an imperfect combination of perfections. Unlike the money-grubbing vulgarity of business, they are perfect in their avowed pursuit of truth and beauty. But they do it in a very imperfect way.

1. CONFLICT/CORRESPONDENCE
OF INTEREST

Taking a hard look at a university is like analyzing a novel or play. Subtexts at each level offer a different meaning. The *level of appearance* displayed in the brochure from the admissions office is cheerful students, devoted faculty, and attentive administrators in a beautiful (if pastoral) or vibrant (if urban) campus.

A correspondence of interests on the appearance level gives way on the *level of operations* to a conflict of interests. Students are more interested in sports and party fun than laboring over their studies, faculty try to get out of teaching to do their "own work" of research, alumni complain about the lousy football team or some Marxist professor, and the local community is pressing to use the basketball court in the gym during the Christmas vacation.

Many service industries, like universities, appear to enjoy a correspondence of interests, but on an operational level are always in danger of a conflict of interest. Architects, lawyers, stockbrokers, real estate agents, and surgeons represent their clients and serve their patients but earn higher fees when the house costs more to build, the case goes to court, the stock is sold/bought, the home is purchased at a higher price, or the patient is wheeled into the operating room.

A conflict of interest on the operational level is a reason why war is too important to be left to the generals, governance to the politicians, business to the managers, hospitals to the physicians, and education to the faculty. The generals, politicians, executives, physicians and professors *begin to run the enterprise for themselves* rather than for the nation, the voters, the shareholders, the patients, or the students.

In universities, professors want to do research on their own projects at convenient times under productive conditions for national and international recognition. "In the push for external recognition, faculty teaching loads are reduced," explains foundation executive Ernest Boyer. "At big universities, freshmen and sophomores often are assigned to large sections, meeting with 'TAs' [teaching assistants]. Undergraduates are

5

especially frustrated when they find themselves trapped in a system where their own interests are put in second place. This adds up to the perception that many institutions are more concerned about status than about their students." Some faculty also moonlight for money, of which consulting is generally the most lucrative. Whether the goal is fame or treasure, teaching undergraduates is secondary.

Just because faculty try to run the shop to benefit their own self-interest doesn't make them different from businessmen. It's only that most people *expect* them to behave differently. The educational mission of the university is not supposed to be about the self-interest of the teacher but the self-development of the students. Teachers do not pursue ambitious personal goals but rather guide others to their goals. Professors belong to the "helping" professions.

People who try to run the organization to benefit themselves are not wicked. You have only to look in the mirror to see that isn't true. Adam Smith's famed eighteenth century advice is instructive: "It is not from the benevolence of the butcher, the brewer, or the baker that we expect our dinner, but from their regard to their own interest. We address ourselves not to their humanity but to their self-love, and never talk to them of our necessities but of their advantages."

In business, hustling for our own self-interest within ethical and legal constructs contributes to the general welfare. At the same time American society is constructed on Judaic-Christian values. So, a tension is created between promoting the selfishness of the self and attending to the needs of others, between working for me and mine and reaching out to thee and thine. The eighteenth century founder of Methodism, John Wesley, put it succinctly: "Gain all you can, save all you can, give all you can." We indirectly give by taking for ourselves; we directly give by offering ourselves through the charity of money and the volunteering of time.

While the tension between the self-seeking demands of capitalism and the self-giving commands of Christianity keep Americans straining to reconcile feelings of guilt, the society works because there is a reluctant, but nonetheless unshakeable conviction, that people will demonstrate an irresistible proclivity towards self-seeking rather than self-giving. Thus, checks and balances, the separation of powers, ballot-box elections, consumer choice, a competitive marketplace, and if they fail, the law and the regulatory powers of the government—all protectively combine to keep the game on the up and up.

Sometimes the system breaks down. Owners may lose control of their property. For example, compliant corporate boards vote huge salary increases to top executives without reference to performance. Average pay for chief executives is often 70 to 80 times greater than the annual wages of the average worker. Indeed, the gap between executives and workers has more than doubled since the mid-1970's. Compared to other economies, chief executives in the United States earn almost twice as much as their counterparts in Canada and Germany—the two nations that rank second and third in chief executive compensation.

The third level, which might be called the *level of results,* is bottom line. Whatever the conflicts of interest—the general's hunger for glory, the politician's passion for power, the businessman's and the physician's drive for money, or the professor's yearning for prestige (or additional income)—wars get won but with a sorrowful loss of life, bills are passed but not always in the public interest, profits grow but not always ethically, patients survive unnecessary operations, and students get degrees albeit secondary in the hierarchy of academic objectives.

On the level of results, the prestigious university delivers. The life-time yield of a baccalaureate from a selective university continues to represent a favorable return on investment. The purpose of the baccalaureate is not so much to lead a richer life spiritually and aesthetically. The aim is to lead a richer life. The tuition-paying parents are investing in a capital asset—the destiny of their child. It's an asset which ranks just behind that other family commitment—the mortgaged home.

It's pretty much a secure lifetime investment, too. Suppliers cannot swiftly move in to meet the demand by creating academic degrees of equivalent desirability. That is one reason why tuition hikes can safely average roughly twice the rate of inflation. Each year tuition increases provoke a litany of lamentations. Parents in a budget squeeze moan while newspapers complain in righteous editorials about irresponsibility. Universities defend the increases by pointing to the labor-intensive nature of their operation or how the federal government cut back on student aid or how foreign journals, indispensable for the library, have skyrocketed in price. A major reason, however, is that *student/parent demand for prestigious degrees exceeds the collegiate supply. There are more aspiring elitists than there are spaces in elite colleges.*

Indeed, participants in the university culture may see a tuition increase above the inflation rate not as a conflict of interest but rather as a correspondence of interest. Buyers (parents/students) are getting more of what they want and so, too, are the sellers (universities/faculty). Faculty scholarship largely determines the academic distinction of the university. A portion of the tuition increase is justified as money to provide faculty with facilities and time to do research. Parents benefit because their child has earned a baccalaureate from a prestigious college that the scholarly faculty has created. Students enter the real world with a marketable degree for a promising career. Faculty, for whom academic prestige is often the sharper spur, publish and are honored by their peers for scholarly eminence. Alumni enjoy equity protection of their degree. "Town" benefits from the flow of income from a secure and sought-after "Gown." The nation recognizes the faculty contributions to knowledge which help to sustain the United States in its position of cultural, scientific, and economic preeminence around the world.

In most occupations there is this correspondence of interest contending with a conflict of interest. How does the rivalry play itself out in the university?

2. MISSION, TRUSTEES, AND THE PRESIDENT

America's 213 doctorate-granting universities boast a robust diversity. (Universities differ from colleges because they include professional schools and may be accredited to offer a Ph.D. degree. Some universities offer only a master's degree.) Massive state systems are distinct from single-campus private universities. Some places corral students into large lectures, grade students by multiple-choice tests, and use graduate students for much of the teaching. There are intimate campuses that fuss over their students. Here faculty actually offer detailed criticisms of student essays, personally grade exams, and care about many of their students like parents in a sharing family.

Our survey population embraces both universities that have arrived and those on the make. Universities with established reputations, and those striving to offer a prestigious undergraduate degree, push for admissions policies that are selective. Their faculties are promoted largely for their research achievements. Still, there is enormous variety from campus to campus, even within the very select group of 58 institutions belonging to the Association of American Universities. When differences are meaningful for specific interpretations, the distinctions are noted.

The 213 doctorate-granting universities, including many highly selective liberal arts colleges, are heirs to a common evaluative tradition. The values that are woven into the texture of their academic culture enjoy a similarity of design. Most universities, and many celebrated colleges, yearn for the prestige which above all is earned by a publishing faculty doing research. *The corporation's "profit center" is the university's "prestige center." The bulls-eye of that prestige center is the scholar.*

Once the potential for academic glory is tasted, the appetite grows on the thing it feeds upon. The old teachers' college strains to move up; the state college pleads for university status. E. Alden Dunham's survey of 279 state colleges discovered that "state college faculties are restive. . . . They jealously look over the fence at the university,

9

where generally higher salaries, better fringe benefits, lighter teaching loads, and greater opportunities for research prevail."

Why the emphasis on scholarship? Howard Bowen and Jack Schuster identified two reasons. "The first is the timeless impulse to emulate the most prestigious universities. As far as we know, no one has tallied the number of institutions claiming to be the Harvard of the South or the Princeton of the West or the Yale of the Midwest, but the total number of such claimants is probably large." The other reason is that there is a supply of potential scholars to meet the demand for institutional distinction. In a buyer's market, universities can select from highly credentialed "young scholars . . . deeply imbued with the research ethos."

Bowen and Schuster concluded in their 1986 study that "many a doctorate-granting university which still falls far short of top rank now explicitly espouses the goal of becoming a leading research university. Such aspirations are not new, but they are now being pursued with single-minded determination. In the groves of academe, to question the importance of research approaches heresy."

The more fervent the pretensions to research excellence, the closer to the prototype described here. To be aware of that grasping but glorious hunger is the point of departure for understanding the nature of the modern university. It also a point of departure for understanding higher education. Research and doctorate-granting universities enjoy a powerful multiplier effect. They produce the college teachers of the future. Ph.Ds carry the value of self-worth defined by scholarship and reinforce it in the colleges that hire them.

The corporate prototype used for comparison is a substantial publicly-owned business. This is a sketch of insights painted with a *very* broad brush. Allowances should be made for institutional variations, regional distinctions, and value nuances in both the business and academic prototypes. The analysis is more critical of higher education, not because the structure/function of business is necessarily more laudable, but because the objective is to understand the culture of the university.

Let us begin at the beginning by defining the goals of a corporation to understand more clearly the objectives of a university.

Mission

What is the purpose of business? It's to make a profit. The objective is to increase earnings per share with a favorable return on investment. The aim is to maximize shareholder wealth. Of course large corporations differ in the style of their culture. Some favor long-term goals. Others press for short-term gains at the expense of strategic growth. Others accept lower earnings for higher *pro bono publico* prestige. Still, with all their differences, businesses share at least two absolutes—meet quarterly expenditures and make a profit, or show a potential for it.

What is the purpose of the university? Colleges and universities embark on what is known as a "mission." Mission, a religious word much favored in the evangelical glossary, implies a pursuit nobler than money, a motivation purer than self-interest. The problem of the university is that it "does good" by following two missions which often collide rather than complement. The result is a purpose clouded in ambiguity.

Universities transmit the culture from one generation to the next by teaching. At the same time they contribute to knowledge through research. The faculties of the universities are charged with both responsibilities. The ambiguity begins with universities professing both missions to be of equal importance. However, scholarly research is the most important criterion for measuring institutional eminence. So, those universities that are determined to be contenders for national recognition promote faculty who can expand the prestige of the university. Faculty who teach undergraduates advance in rank, not on the basis of their competence in teaching, but on the basis of their contributions to knowledge through published research. And that is why *university teaching is the only profession in which you can become a success without satisfying the client.*

How is academic standing of a university measured? The published quality of the faculty is paramount. Other criteria evaluate the quality of the matriculated students. What were their scores on the Scholastic Aptitude Test or the American College Testing Assessment? Where did they stand compared to the other graduates in their high school class? To assess a college's drawing power, what was the acceptance rate, i.e., the ratio of acceptances to applications? What was the enrollment yield, i.e., how many acceptances actually accepted or went elsewhere? To suggest instructional quality, what is the ratio of teachers to students and how many teachers have a Ph.D.? Additional objective, quantitative information might include per-student endowment and how much is spent on library resources. Finally, and crucial, is the subjective, qualitative opinion about academic reputation flowing from various sources—presidents, deans, and professors at other institutions, executive directors who disburse government and foundation grants, the press, opinion-makers, and the public.

Some History

The puissance of published research did not always command policy in the prestigious institutions of higher education. The colonial colleges in the seventeenth and eighteenth centuries began by emulating British models. Teaching was a sacred calling charged with the responsibility of educating young men to be morally upright leaders in the community. The researchers of that time, Thomas Jefferson and Benjamin Franklin, were not academics. Teachers taught what was known. They were not expected to add to knowledge.

For some 250 years, into the closing decades of the nineteenth century, teaching was the commanding objective on the more prestigious campuses. Then, inspired by a new model of the German university, academic energies began to flow into faculty research and the education of graduate students studying for their the Ph.D. degree. By 1894, the University of Chicago's forceful William Rainey Harper laid it on the line to the faculty. "The amount of instruction required by the statutes of the University is comparatively small," he reminded his professors. In a hurry to lift the University of Chicago into international eminence, Harper was hardly discreet in clarifying the prestige hierarchy of teaching and research. It was the duty of the faculty, he decreed, to allocate their time for "that work which in a university must be recognized as higher than instruction—the work of production. . . . No man becomes a member of the University staff of whom great things are not expected. The university will be patient . . . but it expects from every man honest and persistent effort in the direction of contribution to the world's knowledge."

In 1909 the educator Abraham Flexner reported a conversation with a college dean. Who was the best teacher in his college? The dean named a certain instructor:

What is his rank?
Assistant Professor.
When will his appointment expire?
Shortly.
Will he be promoted?
No.
Why not?
He hasn't *done* anything!

As the teacher slid into second-class status, respect for the learned generalist followed the descent. Specialization was the route to a permanent job. Multiplying departments splintered the unity of knowledge. Fields within departments narrowed into protected specialties. In the decades after World War II professors increasingly shifted their loyalties from the university campus to their professional specialties. The academy was moving inexorably away from what historian Frederick Rudolph has called "such older collegiate values as close faculty-student relations, small classes, and attention to oral and written communication."

In the long journey from colonial college to modern university, the mission had expanded to embrace research as well as teaching. One thing did not change. Job applicants were still hired as teachers. What did change was that teachers were evaluated as researchers.

Trustees

Power begins with ownership. The corporate source of power is precise. The corporation is owned by the shareholders. They know what they want from the money they invest—more money. They are not confused by emotional attachments to their equity, though sometimes racial (South Africa) or health (tobacco companies) issues will influence decisions. The only tear a shareholder sheds is when "profit" turns to "loss" in the annual profit and loss contest. Shareholders buy without loyalty and sell without compassion. They select as their representatives a board of directors which they hope will maximize wealth.

Who owns the university? The alumni are convinced they do. Students claim they own a piece of it. The faculty demand a part because they are giving their lives to it. Lately, local communities have been presuming a turf proprietorship. Strict agency bureaucrats claim no proprietorship, but point out that the federal government is not interested in giving to be blessed but to receive contracts on time according to specifications.

The ambiguity of the university is further clouded by the makeup of the board of trustees—who as a body are the actual owners in trust and are sometimes required to affirm it. Private universities settle into the seats of the board of trustees religious leaders, donors, powerful businessmen, popular alumni, at least one attorney (a visible Point of Light for client-seeking rainmakers), perhaps a trusted academic, student

13

activists, and sufficient minorities to calm the protests of special interest groups.

In the corporation, the governing body consists of paid directors, some internal to the company, others from the outside. The president of the company usually chairs the board, combining roles in the corporation kept separate in the university. The corporate board focuses on clearly defined objectives.

In *private* universities, the board of trustees is an uncoordinated, unpaid conglomerate of high achieving individuals in the professions and business who are not always certain what they are supposed to do. What some members do know is that they are expected to acknowledge the honor bestowed upon them by abundant gestures of benevolence.

In *public* universities, members of the board get there by many routes. Some are self-perpetuating, others are appointed by the governor or elected by the state legislature, still others are selected by the alumni. Sunshine laws requiring meetings to be public, with written records made available, don't ease the give and take of decision-making.

Public universities reaffirm the certitude that whenever elective politics gets involved in an operation, procedures become more expensive and decisions more untidy. If the objectives of the university are teaching and research supplemented by service to the community, the objective of the politician is to get reelected. The spending of taxpayer's money foolishly, or corruptly, must be minimized by levels of oversight enforced by layers of a state education bureaucracy. Spending money increasingly costs money.

A caricature of a quarterly trustee meeting might picture it as a pursuit of individual agendas—rather like an assemblage of state legislators. The cleric on the board laments the loss of traditional values, the student weighs in with the current burden of social responsibility, the popular alumnus stands for a winning football team, the minority representative presses for ghetto recruitment, the academic representative talks of standards, the business executive isolates the budget, and the political appointees are fingering likely candidates to blame should something go wrong. It's a chaos of voting motivations with contending educational objectives crisscrossing in an atmosphere in which civility blessedly rules as confusion unwillingly prevails. The scenario is a caricature, of course. The meetings are disciplined and conflicts are usually resolved in smaller committees. Still, university trustees, both private and public, reflect the values of diverse constituencies while corporate

14

directors are supposed to represent the interests of profit-seeking share-holders.

The President

In most corporations, future presidents are assigned early in their careers to on-the-job training for leadership. The route to the top is measured by a sequence of promotions. At each step the promising executive is tested and moves up. The mobility process often takes place within the same corporation, and generally in enterprises within the same industry. It takes decades and involves specific training, additional educational preparation, and incessant performance evaluations. When the board of directors selects the chief executive officer, they have chosen someone who has been trained, tested, and motivated to be the boss.

In colleges and universities presidents train to be chief executive officers, not by handling the coinage of budgets and bottom lines, but by being a teacher and scholar. They are trained for three or more years in graduate school to be a scholar. Then they teach. Promotion to full professor is not for competence at running things but for excellence in research. The first encounter with management may be as departmental chairperson. The choice is then a return to full-time teaching/research or on to the dean's office.

Today it is almost respectable to seek the presidency of a college; just a few short years ago it was considered bad form. Indeed, duplicity is not now unknown. A search consultant was working with a small Catholic college to find the right president and advertised the position. In the mail came a letter that began: "Dear Sir: I am a devout Catholic. . . ." Several months later the consultant was searching for a president, this time for a Calvinist college. In the stack of applications was a letter from Guess Who: "Dear Sir: I am a devout Calvinist."

Not long ago presidents of universities were "called" much like ministers, for it was, indeed, the ministry that shaped many of the values surrounding the academic profession. If it was God's will that the leader should lay down the things he or she loved for the heavy burdens of administration, the sacrifice would be made.

Mock the pretense, but there is often pain. In business, executives keep managing to higher levels of responsibility. In the academy, there is a dichotomy in the mobility route. Teaching/research are different kinds of work—totally different—from administration. So, the sad tale of presidents is that climbing the administrative ladder decrees the abandonment of the kind of work they entered the occupation to do in the first place.

The president's faculty colleagues summon no empathy for that kind of pain. The president has sold out, like those gifted novelists capitulating to Hollywood. The payoffs are power, status, the mansion, and servants. In the faculty's hierarchy of prestige, pinnacles of achievement are earned by personal qualities that *really* count. Such a pinnacle is the presidency of a professional association—the American Historical Association, say, or the American Sociological Association.

The irony for the faculty, of course, is that the president must be one of their own, even though he or she has joined the alien camp of administration. The president must have been tested by the doctorate ordeal, suffered before the blank piece of paper or before the exasperating laboratory experiment, graded disappointing examinations, dozed through faculty meetings, and sweated through the ego-threatening finality of the tenure process that results in no job at all or a guaranteed income for life.

It is probably true that every occupation wants its leaders to have paid their dues in the coinage of its own suffering. In business, however, the training for leadership begins at the entry level. And the CEO may be feared but is not rebuffed into an alien camp. In the academy, the training for administrative leadership begins much later, if at all. And the president is estranged.

Why is the life of the teacher-scholar so different from the work of the administrator? The teacher-scholar delights in the flirtatious play of ideas, believes in learning for learning's sake, reveres art for its cherished self, and respects above all the truth revealed by a defensible methodology. The teacher-scholar is seldom required decisively to select among alternative courses of action and then stick with it. The administrator, on the other hand, must define criteria, isolate the options, establish priorities, and then make decisions within the context of a nagging budget. The teacher-scholar is incessantly abstracting towards the truth; the administrator must decide on options for a doable course of action. The teacher-scholar is delighted by process; the administrator is plagued by consequences.

16

3. THE EXERCISE OF AUTHORITY

Who exercises authority? Walk into corporate headquarters and ask: "Who's in charge here?" You will be sent to the office of the chief executive officer. Business enterprises are hierarchical organizations with lines to the apex of pyramidal power. The president or the chairman of the board, with the approval of the board of directors, ultimately decides what product is to be manufactured or service offered, who is to do it, who is to be promoted and who to be fired. It is true that the vertical hierarchy of command is shifting to a more horizontal flow. The CEO may indeed be more like the conductor of a symphony orchestra with employees knowing the score than the more traditional general of the army with the troops following orders through a chain of command. Open-door offices and quality circles may encourage employee creativity. Still, with all the loosening up through a democratization of the workplace, the CEO is the boss with the authority to support the responsibilities of office.

Walk onto a university campus and ask: "Who's in charge here?" The answer will depend upon whom you ask. Let us assume, for a sharper comparison, that you chance upon the faculty pit bull. He will pause long enough on the way to class to confess that he really doesn't understand what the question means. He will explain, though, that he and his departmental colleagues decide what is to be taught and who is to teach it. Further, they decide who is to be promoted. They also decide, with their colleagues in other departments, which students will graduate and with what honors. Still, a visitor might reply: "Surely there is someone in charge who is responsible." The professor will ponder for what may seem an uncomfortable period of time and then call over his disappearing shoulder: "The president's office is over there. He's the housekeeper and fund raiser."

A freshly minted university president offers an echo. "A funny thing happened to me on the way to the presidency of the University of Hartford," reported Stephen Joel Trachtenberg. Trachtenberg endured long interviews with various university constituencies. He was invited to

17

tell the faculty "at enormous length about my opinions, feelings, intuitions and preferences in matters of teaching, research, learning, and scholarship. This part of the interview process, I must confess, I rather welcomed, since it implied that as president I would be expected to concern myself with the very activities that distinguish a university from other corporate or government endeavors. As it turned out, I was sadly mistaken. No sooner had I been inaugurated than I found that attempts on my part to actively participate in these professorial activities was regarded with the same favor as a tap-dancer at a funeral. The first role of a university president, I was informed in no uncertain terms, is to bring the school to the attention of people with money in their pockets."

A mendicant in a mansion, the university president does exercise some power. It begins with time and money. The appointment calendar governs time. Shrewd presidents knowingly, or instinctively, decide how much of their time is to be spent with individuals with whom they share power, mostly the faculty, and how much time is to be spent with those who can exert power over them by making decisions favorable to the university—or to their personal careers. Topping that list are influential trustees, rich alumni, foundation executives, and above all the press.

The power of the president is also exercised in the shaping of the budget. The president sets the salaries of the faculty with the approval of the trustees. There is leverage in that authority. Of course when revenues are abundant, everyone is a hero. In a more turf-sensitive, steady-state budget, the degree to which resources can be reallocated is largely determined by the percentage of faculty who are "tenured in." On the downside, in a fiscal crisis, presidents do miraculously survive. It's a time when the loyalty of faculty supporters is tested. As anyone knows who has sat at the place where the buck stops, the beneficence of an expanding budget will boast a thousand fathers; a giveback compelled by shrinking revenues is an orphan!

The less prestigious the university, the more powerful the president. In the drive to make their university a national research center, presidents collect about them forceful faculty with doctorates earned at distinguished institutions. The irony is that the degree to which presidents succeed in putting their universities on the academic map is the degree to which the power of the presidency in relation to the faculty is diminished.

"Held Together by a Central Heating System"

A university is a conglomerate of knowledge. The basic organizational unit is the department. Decision making is decentralized into some 25
to 35 departments which are further reduced to "fields." While fields are
modified and interdisciplinary programs ebb and flow according to the
fashion of the times, the long-term commitment of the university in
space, equipment, books, and people is to the department.

Decision-making in the academy is largely collegial. Collective
responsibility is expressed through the decisions of committees. Decisions by committees, alas, too easily drift into irresponsibility because
accountability is spread over so many individuals. Like legislatures, they
are tempted to protect the interests of constituencies rather than the
long-term objectives of the institution. Faculty power expressed in the
collegial concept of collective responsibility can result in presidential
accountability for decisions that the president and board of trustees were
unable to control. Responsibility for consequences is thus severed from
the authority to control the decisions that produced the consequences.

Business executives are keyed to current management training that
nurtures team-building. They are specialists but are required to coordi-
nate their work. It is a foolish head of manufacturing who does not ask for
feedback from the sales division in shaping design attractiveness.

By contrast, a modern university resists cooperative effort. The
University of Chicago's Robert Maynard Hutchins was reported to have
described a modern university as "a series of separate schools and departments held together by a central heating system." Faculty are specialists
who work in departments unrelated to each other. And as knowledge
accumulates, specialization further narrows the fields within departments. So, while business executives are forced to become team players,
academics are rewarded for being individualists who work mostly in
solitude.

In the 1980 *Yeshiva University* decision on collegiality, the Supreme
Court put the force of law behind the reality of shared governance. The
court declared that the faculty of Yeshiva, a private institution, was not
entitled to bargain collectively because they were part of management.
Later court rulings have confirmed that faculties in private institutions
may not organize because they play a predominant role in the hiring,
tenure, termination, and promotion of their colleagues as well as exercis-
ing substantial authority in such policy matters as curriculum, grading,
teaching methods, student discipline, and course schedules.

19

Crisis Management and Damage Control

Compared to a business enterprise, the exercise of authority in a university culture is enormously complicated. After working all day, business employees go home. The campus of a residential university *is* home. The persistence of Latinate terms—*Alma Mater* and *in loco parentis*—formally testify to the campus as a nourishing mother serving in the role of parents. Faithful alumni return for a "Homecoming." A residential university *is* family.

Just as the power of teenagers in the American family has increased, so has the power of students on American campuses. The mighty heave for delegated power on campus began in the 1960's. Students demanded their share. What they discovered was not very much power lying around. What was available beat not to the bolero of exhilarating revolution but to the minuet of protocol.

Students are now a part of the administrative process. Presidents at one time unilaterally, but with faculty consultation, selected their own deans. Now search committees frequently include student representatives who offer candidates, usually three, from which the president makes a choice. The addition of the student dimension to administration, alas, increases the need for administrators. Thus do revolutions often produce the very consequences revolutionary leaders deplore.

Power to some extent is exercised by students in their formal representation on committees and legislative bodies. But the real wallop, if measured in terms of its consequences for their suffering surrogate parents, is in what is known as "extracurricular activities." What takes place outside the classroom is made more volatile by the increasing diversity of the student body. Blacks, Hispanics, and Asians, gays, women, and the handicapped join the traditional mix of political radicals and right-wingers to induce a mood of dread anticipation in the Office of the Dean of Student Affairs. Deans of Student Affairs have the right to wonder why their office should be held accountable for undergraduate behavior which they often do not have the authority to control. In that sense *in loco parentis* is probably not much different from acting as the real parent.

The responsibility for authority on university campuses has become an exercise in crisis management. When preventive measures falter, it's damage control. Sure, corporate CEO's are occasionally hit with a tanker spill, trusted vice-presidents bribe government officials, and poisoned products materialize on supermarket shelves. But that is nothing compared to the emotional volatility of student consumers daily and nightly clustered in one location and churning with complex emotional feelings about parental surrogates.

An undergraduate body is, far more than it used to be, an agitation of special interest groups. Conservative broadsides are calling for a white student center. Should a white student center be funded or should the black student center be phased out? What is the university's position on "straight pride?" Should faculty candidates for hiring, promotion, and tenure with Hispanic-sounding surnames be given preferential consideration? Was it acceptable behavior for a female journalism student to go topless as a singing-telegram stripper in order to get a investigative story on a local flesh peddler? How more hypocritical can it get than when the Board of Trustees refuses to divest tobacco industry stocks in the endowment portfolio while at the same time voting to ban smoking in school buildings? Posting a centerfold photograph from *Penthouse* in a coed dormitory is offensive to many women, hanging a Confederate flag for all to see is an assault on black sensitivity—but doesn't the First Amendment guarantee . . . ?

The danger for the university is that damage control is no longer confined to mediating a family fight. Charges of racism, sexism, homophobiaism, pharisaism, authoritarianism, not to mention accusations of political extremism corrupting academic objectivity in the classroom, can leach into the "outside" world. There, ideological advocates or professional ethnics are in wait to pick up the cause. Now the strategy must defend the reputation of the university against the bullying of national press coverage. The damage to be contained is no longer manipulated by amateur students. Now they are united in solidarity with paid professionals. The professionals keep the issue alive, not only because they believe in the justice of their cause, but because that is the way they earn their living. Campus damage control is like fighting a fire while students keep finding ways to turn off the water supply as ideologically sympathetic professors cheer them on.

Similar to the irony of university presidents who diminish their own power on campus by building a strong research faculty is the irony of presidents who diligently searched for qualified blacks to rectify past injustices of admissions access. The degree to which they tried to "do good" by increasing the percentage of blacks on campus was the degree to which some had created an unsuspected cauldron of social discontent. The racial turmoil threatened the president's own job security.

Every bureaucrat, especially in government, knows that innovative leadership is risky. Job security resides in doing less rather than more. Innovation augments the chances for a backfiring disaster, especially when the media is constantly reminded in press releases about the university's "can-do" leadership. A high profile sculptured by the public affairs office invites the president and the university to be newsworthy. Just as fresh infusions to the endowment or appointment to a task force claim media coverage, so too do indignant gays picketing the president's office, drunken students deflowering a maiden in a fraternity house, or a booster in a secluded garage handing over the keys of a sports car to the football captain. Thus with the commendable intent of promoting their enterprise do university presidents author the misfortune of uninvited reporters.

Sports

Not all extracurricular activities complicate the exercise of authority. Well . . . there's the stamp club, though on some campus at this very moment students are probably flirting with the thrill of printing their own. One extracurricular activity that is difficult to control, because on some campuses it is out of control, is athletics, especially the major sports of football and basketball.

Athletics are not covered in this study. Major universities share a common *academic* culture but are markedly different in the *athletic* aspects of that culture. The difference is not in the ardor for victory, which they all share, but the means tolerated to achieve victory. While faculty values are interchangeable in prestigious institutions, the faculty does not control athletic directors and coaches. Thus, generalizations about university culture must exclude the athletic dimension.

One issue about athletics, however, is worth introducing even though applicable to only some prestigious universities. University presidents are supposed to exist in an ivory tower protected from worldly temptations; business executives must daily endure the ethical strain of shady means applied for profitable ends. There is no misfortune more piteous than presidents of universities, mostly public with state or city names, trapped in the nightmare of athletic ends corrupting academic means.

These presidents must exercise their authority on campuses as they slouch towards a betrayal of ideals while hazarding the scandal of exposure. The shame is an index of educational perversions—"greasing"

22

academically unqualified athletes through the admissions office and into "gut" courses, expecting jocks to practice excessive hours with road trips while still attending classes and doing the assigned reading, adjusting academic standards to athletic prowess, exploiting "black gladiators" with the thumbs down of low graduation rates, paying coaches with nicknames like "Gunslinger" and "The Shark" exorbitant salaries while they endorse products, permitting coaches in the name of the university to patrol the sidelines like ranting lunatics. Victory under such circumstances must be a melancholy satisfaction for those believing that a liberal arts education and amateur sports in concert are graced with a special harmony.

As sportscasters are wont to phrase it, you have to ask yourself: If some universities are in the business of commercial entertainment, why not disassociate major sports from formal education? Players do not have to be students; they would be paid. In that way the university's major sports can serve as a farm club, somewhat like baseball, while charging professional teams for training their rookies. The rest of the undergraduate body can do battle in intramural or less formal intercollegiate programs—the kind that end the contest with competing teams having dinner together in camaraderie. Should the pay-for-play professionals on the farm team wish to earn credits, they can enroll part-time. Alumni and student fans can cheer with slam-dunk exuberance in a school spirit similar to the enthusiasm bestowed on their favorite professional football, basketball, baseball, and hockey teams.

If models similar to this were to evolve, predicts sports critic Murray Sperber, "there would be a great collective sigh of relief in American higher education," not to mention in locker rooms where jocks would feel better about an honest paycheck. Then, as the saying goes, they can truly help build a university of which the football team may be proud.

Still, as the sportscasters also recite, you gotta believe when a garland of "poet-athletes" at Harvard gathered round to read their poetry to an invited audience. Mike Betsy, a football offensive guard, delivered his "Ode to Shelley" to a more immediate Shelley—Shelley McDonough, his girlfriend in the audience:

Oh Shelley
My love for you is as eternal as the stars in the sky,
Or so I wish.
But alas, I must see through the guise and know
That all things must come to pass.

Oh Shelley my love for you is like a ripened fruit on the vine.
It is a beautiful sight to gaze upon from afar,
Yet once picked, time becomes precious.
For though the fruit of love is sweet,
We are always left with the pits.

But if pits are treated with love and affection,
They can blossom into Mother Nature's perfection,
And our tree can bear the thing
That only my lovely Shelley can bring.

Is there a more seductive way to woo a Shelley . . . ?

A Hierarchy of Unequal Equals

A university president exercises authority through persuasion rather than edict. The task is to hold together splintering constituencies. There are the special interest claims of blacks, gays, and the handicapped, women and environmentalists. As noted earlier, there are alumni outraged by a football team fumbling its way to losses which some prefer to identify with a failure of masculinity. Some students are plotting extra-curricular capers while others plan to mount a defense of (or attack on) an extremist professor. The surrounding community is plenty disgusted with student behavior while the faculty is resisting administrative reforms.

University presidents do have at least one advantage over corporate CEOs. That advantage, along about mid-winter, begins to loom more invitingly with each passing month. In late spring, and none too soon, it's commencement. That's when students depart, faculty disperse, and serenity approaches. Alas, too brief is summer's sweet hiatus. The fall term begins with persistent problems too often joined by additional afflictions. Clark Kerr, when he was chancellor of the University of California at Berkeley, identified three: "I have come to the conclusion that there are three great problems at Berkeley and they are: sex for the students, athletics for the alumni and parking for the faculty."

Rarely does a businessman head a major college. David T. McLaughlin is an exception. He moved from CEO of the Toro Company, a lawnmower manufacturer, to the presidency of Dartmouth. "The college presidency is more. time-demanding and more emotionally demanding than anything I experienced in the corporate world," he explained. "It's not just the pluralism of lots of constituencies. There's

24

almost a preoccupation with the process of decision-making, as opposed to the decision itself." McLaughlin went on to point out that running an academic institution was closer to political governance than corporate management. "The fundamentals of administration—accounting, planning and so forth—are the same as in the business world, but the consensus-building is different. In academia, you spend huge amounts of time deciding what to do . . . ." That's what politicians in legislatures do. It's one reason why politicians make safer university presidents than businessmen—though the faculty resists the selection of both the one and the other.

Authority in the academy is exercised by a hierarchy of unequal equals that is designed to express opinions rather than to execute the decisiveness of command.

4. THE FACULTY

Nowhere are the dissimilarities between corporations and universities more pronounced than in the their key personnel. Business is flexible in the hiring/firing, pay, and work loads of executives. The academy is rigid. Faculty are tenured, now in some institutions over 80%, representing an investment incapable of change. The purpose of tenure is protection of intellectual freedom; the consequence is job security. A life-tenured professor can represent a fixed investment in excess of one million dollars spanning over a quarter of a century.

Tenured faculty are unfortunately not assets that can be sold in the marketplace. They can only be purchased. Professors, alas, are not football players who can be traded. (We offer two heavily published authorities in Political Science, where we are deep in the bench, for your promising professor of Physics.) Professors, on the other hand, are free to take a more attractive job. Indeed, many prestigious institutions offer two-year leaves of absence to their faculty who may return if dissatisfied with the job jump. The university, on the other hand, is bound by a virtually irrevocable commitment to pay tenured professors for life until retirement. It is an arrangement that some businessmen may find bewildering until it is understood that regulations governing the faculty are not made by their employers but by the faculty.

It is possible to overemphasize the importance of the tenure decision in the life of an academic—but few observers have been able to do it. For the straining assistant professor it's up or out. "Up" to associate professor and the bliss of lifetime security; "out" to perilous financial insecurity.

One way to feed the family is to fill in for an absent professor. They're the gypsies hustling for next year's job while meeting this year's classes. More unhappy than these annual nomads are the adjunct commuters. They travel to various campuses as adjunct teachers, subcontractors really, and are paid an impoverishing hourly wage without fringe benefits.

In the criteria for tenure—scholarly achievement (with further promise), teaching effectiveness, and contribution to the operations of the university, e.g., committee work—scholarly publication is of course the most important of the forbidding trio. It all begins with the doctoral dissertation—an eternal exercise which endows patience with the virtue of divine grace.

With doctorate earned and teaching begun in a "tenure track" appointment, the dread mounts as the tenure decision looms. Key is a published book. Authors in search of a publisher frequently become sophisticated direct mail merchandisers. The problem is that incipient scholars can't get their books published by paying for it themselves. Publishers, both commercial and university presses, shrink at the accusation of being tagged as vanity houses.

Are there options? Not many, but a hypothetical will point up the importance of tenure. How much money is tenure worth as a lifetime payoff, assuming that the candidate would not be happy in another line of work? If the university gave the assistant professor a letter of intent stating that the manuscript published as a book would virtually guarantee a tenure appointment, if the supplicant found a reputable publisher who was willing to publish the book for a negotiated fee, and if the gleeful aspirant went to the bank for a loan using the letter as collateral, how much money should be borrowed to pay the publisher in order to make the deal financially sound? We'll leave it to the accountants to come up with a figure using average salary scales, but the answer is: "Plenty!"

What a Neat Way to Cut Costs

While universities are decentralized into departments defined by subject matter, e.g., philosophy and mathematics, corporations are decentralized into units defined by function, e.g., manufacturing, sales, and finance. As corporation executives climb the career ladder, they do different kinds of work with different kinds of responsibilities. The paycheck for sixty year old executives will be four or five times greater than what they were pulling down at the age of thirty-five. In a university, associate professors at the age of thirty-five will be full professors at age sixty doing pretty much the same kind of work they did twenty-five years earlier. Classes may contain more advanced students and working hours in the classroom a bit less, but research will be carried forward with the same procedures and the paycheck most likely will not even have doubled.

28

Indeed, in the university the value of a student credit is the same whoever teaches the class. Surely, one is compelled to ask, a credit given by a graduate student, doubling as a teaching assistant, is not awarded the *same value* as a credit by a distinguished professor holding an endowed chair? Well, if that is the case, and it is, why not hire cheaper labor to do the same job? An hourly adjunct, or a teaching assistant, can stand before the same class as a full professor three times a week for 15 weeks for a total of 45 hours and the value of the credits awarded by each is the same. Hey, what a great way to reduce costs!

Suppose the value of a credit was assessed by the experience and rank of the teacher? Playful investigators will be enticed into speculating on the consequences of what would happen if that were the way it worked. Quality in the delivery of the university's service should improve. The price of a credit would skyrocket. Parents would have to rent a tractor-trailer to transport tuition to the Registrar!

Universities can save money by "churning"—to borrow from the stockbrokers' lexicon. Churning by a stockbroker is trading a customer's securities excessively in order to earn more in commissions. In the academy, it is repeatedly bringing in assistant professors to teach for five years or so and then firing them. The university avoids the risk of awarding tenure to an assistant professor who over endless decades might fail to publish.

Luring established scholars from other universities is a safer method of sustaining a research reputation—though many a campus has regretted the raid when the scholar's creative juices immediately dried to an occasional book review.

Would it not be more just if the academy followed the procedures of business? Departing business executives leave behind the profits they earned for the abandoned company. One might assume that departing scholars would leave their scholarly distinction to the university that paid them where the research was done. That's not the way it works. The investment is wiped out when the scholar decamps in disloyal flight to another campus. *Scholars take their eminence with them.* They're kind of like free agents who also enjoy a guaranteed place in the starting line-up.

Mischievous observers may yield to speculating once again. What would happen in the rivalry for academic distinction if the university claimed its rightful ownership and eminence did not travel with the departing scholar but tarried where it was paid for?

What would happen if faculty were treated like coaches? Well, the power of the students over their teachers would be fearfully magnified. If athletes don't win for their coach, the coach gets fired. If graduating students didn't win for their teachers by scoring high in exams for entrance to professional schools, their teacher would get fired! Only kidding, of course.

"I Have the Freedom . . . ."

Employee tasks and time are managed differently in corporations and universities. Business executives are assigned specific jobs and working time is regimented throughout the week with tight controls. Faculty, on the other hand, enjoy more flexibility in job assignments. "I worked on Wall Street for a time," recalled the economist Burton G. Malkiel, "and I enjoyed it. But the beauty of being at a university is that I have the freedom to decide what I'm going to work on and, to a large extent, what I'm going to teach."

Faculty are also awarded huge amounts of discretionary time. A new chancellor in a state-wide educational system, innocent of the customs of the academy, asked if the professors were in their offices and classrooms from 9 to 5 every day. A not unreasonable question for business but an incongruous one for the academy. A newly appointed trustee to the board of a university asked how many hours the faculty taught and was informed 9 hours. "It's a long day," he replied, "but at least the work is interesting."

How many hours do faculty actually labor? A teaching "load" of 6 to 9 hours per week, plus 3 office hours for student advising, and several hours for committee work can comfortably be accomplished in 2 1/2 days. In addition to the free time of the other 2 1/2 days there are summer vacation and holiday breaks of four months which may be filled with golf, fooling around with a hobby, or just loafing. And the paycheck is guaranteed until age 65 when a dependable TIAA/CREF pension (or the equivalent) eases the transition into fulltime leisure.

While such a lifestyle is possible, it's not an academic career that the committees recommending tenure had in mind. The ideal is that the free 2 1/2 days a week, and at least three of the four holiday/vacation months, are to be spent in research and publication. The reality is that tenured professors enjoy immense freedom in the use of discretionary time.

Individual variations in professorial productivity, measured by teaching load, scholarly achievement, and contributions to the operation of the university, are far greater in the academy than productivity equivalents in business. Some associate professors, awarded tenure after seven years, begin a lifetime of exhausting sixty-hour workweeks teaching undergraduates, advising doctoral students, serving on committees, and contributing new knowledge and interpretations to their field. Others more modestly keep up with the literature in their field and faithfully serve the varied needs of campus life. Still others settle back into a lifetime of goofing off by repeating the same course material every year, ducking committee assignments, and avoiding students.

The irony in faculty workloads is a presumption of roughly equal contributions confronting the reality of vastly unequal effort and results. The ideal assumption is that all professors in the faculty will contribute to knowledge and do so pretty much within a narrow range of achievement. The reality is that there are extreme differences within the same university in the published productivity of the faculty.

If the ideal were limited to top universities, the consequences would be insignificant for higher educational productivity. The ideal spreads like an oil slick. The assumption is that given shrewd administrators and sufficient money a university can become a player. Reducing the time spent teaching undergraduates creates a level playing field for the faculty in competition with other faculties across the nation. Less time with undergraduates means more time for research. The result is the anticipation of more scholarly publications resulting in national recognition.

When the aspiring university declares itself to be a player in contention, a price must be paid. The hunger for national recognition diverts resources from the mission of education to the mission of research. The consequences are a reduction in productivity because faculty teaching loads are driven down equally within departments while scholarly contributions are unequal. The result is an imbalance. The differential scholarly contributions of some cannot compensate for the equal teaching loads of all.

Another price to be paid is the increasing use of graduate students as teaching assistants. They're inexperienced, of course, but like their mentors they share a dual loyalty. If they know what's good for themselves, they will do their "own work" and get the doctorate rather than nurture other minds.

The most painful price of all—higher tuition if a private university, higher taxes for everyone if a state system.

Consulting

Among the thousands of tenured professors in the more prestigious universities are the SuperStars. They serve as consultants or write textbooks. They speak not of honorariums but of fees, not of fixed payments but of escalating royalties. Like popular musicians and winning athletes, they have become successful without the need of venture capital. Their capital is in their SuperStar selves, not in a physical plant burdened with overhead. They are the academy's wheelers and dealers with incomes which can mushroom into the substantial six figures.

Harvard University president Derek Bok was clearly concerned about the trend. For many scholars, Bok explained in the mid-1980's, the growing opportunities for consulting, government service, and contacts with the public represent "for many professors a mounting source of excitement, variety, status and income. . . . In a world that honors success and opulent life styles, we could easily find ourselves harboring more and more professors who try to combine the freedom and security of a tenured academic post with the income and visibility traditionally reserved for people who take much greater risks and work at much less elevating tasks."

Most institutions limit the outside work of the faculty. Let's take the Big Three of the Ivy League which are often regarded as models. At Harvard, outside work is formally limited to no more than 20% of a professor's total professional effort during the academic year. At Yale, it's on the average no more than one day per seven-day week in any academic semester. At Princeton, it's no more than an average of one day a calendar week during the academic year (vacations excluded).

With a school year of eight months, one day a week would add up to another month free for actual on-site work at an office or plant. So, the professor could teach seven months and work at an outside income for five months of the year. The calculation does not include weekends or sabbaticals. But who's counting? Regulatory agencies at universities, if any, are generally weak. Mostly professors report to the departmental chairperson recording their own time or per cent of professional effort devoted to outside work.

The scenario describes the SuperStars, limited to a small minority on the faculties of prestigious universities. Most are in the social sciences (e.g., economists) or the natural sciences (e.g., chemists); few are numbered in the humanities. Some philosophers, musicologists, and art critics have found a marketable niche, but not often with Kant, Bach, and Boticelli as vendible candidates.

A theory of earnings assumes that jobs with high security and high prestige (academic) would have low pay. Jobs with higher risk and lower prestige (advertising) would pay more. The theory is that the higher the justification for work done (the ministry), the lower the pay; the higher the risk (oil drilling), the higher the pay. In the light of such a theory of earnings, the concern of Harvard's President Bok bears repeating about the fidelity of "more and more professors who try to combine the freedom and security of a tenured academic post with the income and visibility traditionally reserved for people who take much greater risks and work at much less elevating tasks."

There is one solution to consulting. Since professors are paid for a full-time job (teaching, research, and service), and since they use university facilities such as an office, telephone, and maybe even a proposal letter duplicated on the departmental copying machine, the fees they receive should be signed over to their employer. You think we're kidding? The University of Chicago (where else) for some years required newly appointed faculty to remit their earned outside income to the university. What do you suppose the total revenues would amount to if the professors at, say, MIT were required to sign over their consulting checks to the Vice-president for Financial Operations? Enough to decrease appreciably the price of undergraduate tuition?

In any case, SuperStars, and many faculty with incomes from more modest fees and royalties, continue to differ from equally successful achievers in business in two ways. They get paid for pursuing multiple goals and deposit paychecks from multiple sources. Campus critics, yearning for a time when learning seemed more gentle and taste more refined, can only be grateful that no one has reported, at least yet, overhearing a SuperStar opine: "Have your people talk to my people."

Measuring Personal Worth

It is a folk assumption that college teachers are driven by higher motives than business executives. It is purifying to believe that altruistic motives are more likely to flourish in education than in business. It is comforting for teachers to assume that in their low-paying profession they are driven less by self-seeking. Rather, they are assumed to find their satisfaction in a self-giving devotion to the molding of young men and women. At one time the teaching profession was associated in the

33

public mind with religion and shared some of the purity of the spiritual impulse. The impulse has been secularized but still sustains the sacrificial justification by being filed under the career-guidance rubric of the "helping professions."

However noble the calling of teacher, research breakthroughs in the laboratory, one suspects, do not flow solely from an impulse to "do good" but from an ego striving to assert the self through research. Just so in business where entrepreneurial innovations are not driven solely by greed but by an ego thrust to appease the dissatisfied consumer within the entrepreneurial breast.

The difference is in the payoff—for the executive, it's money as a way of keeping score; for the scientist/scholar, it's prestige. *Achievement for both measures personal worth.* And both are illustrations of how a society, to be at the same time productive and free, must organize self-interest so that it adds up to the general good.

For most of us life consists of little triumphs—like remembering to floss or discovering that we are loveable to someone we love. For those with destinies, life consists of doing what either deserves to be written about or writing what deserves to be read. A supreme reward for a scholar is a respected peer testifying in print that the research done deserved to be read.

That supreme reward may be in the process of a redefinition. Is business seducing a compliant university? Is the pursuit of truth for its own sake being overtaken by the rush for money? Is the openness of inquiry in the natural sciences being snapped shut by the secrecy of patent pending? Sir John Kendrew, a Nobel laureate in biology at England's Cambridge University, put the growing problem in international perspective: "Traditionally, science has been an open subject. But now there is a change, even within national communities of scientists, and in particular biologists. Nowdays they don't talk to one another so freely, because each feels that his research may be important industrially—in other words, that there may be money in it, and specifically money in it for him or her."

It may be that the New World Order is nation vs. nation in a battle for economic supremacy, university vs. university in a contest for revenue, and professor vs. professor for a rightful share. In that case, ascending to the presidency of the scientific association may seem less desirable (particularly for the stay-at-home spouse paying family bills) than assuming the presidency of a lucrative research corporation—time limited to one day a week when school is in session, of course. Pure research for prestige vs. applied research for profits is a tormenting issue for the academy.

Federal funding has become crucial for not only scholars but their universities. Howard Cosell (you know him as the sportscaster) prompted A. Bartlett Giamatti to tell it like it is not long after Giamatti had retired from the presidency of Yale:

> Howard, people just don't understand that the real big-time, the real big money that comes into research universities, is not from sports but from the federal research money, and that is the money that supports the schools, not sports revenue.
>
> Would you elaborate?
>
> Certainly. Let's say a school gets one million dollars from the Defense Department for research. That one million goes to support the real costs of doing the research, the light for the rooms, the heat, the air-conditioning—the basics. Then you get what's called indirect recovery money to support the research, and that's sixty-five percent to seventy-two percent above the million. The kind of money I'm talking about swamps the big-time college sports money. And all the big-time schools get this research money, ever since the Manhattan Project. And it's that money which is necessary for a university's sustenance; it's that money which builds the library or new laboratories.

But more of that later.

Scholars contribute to knowledge. University-based research has contributed in a significant way to making the United States technologically superior, militarily supreme, and culturally preeminent. While there are think-tanks and self-contained institutes, much of the research in the past decades that has propelled America into scientific *and* cultural prominence has emerged from major campuses. From bioenergetics and computer software through literary criticism to sociological analysis it has been mostly the professors ducking undergraduate teaching who have made the contributions. In the humanities and social sciences the motivation has largely been prestige. In the natural sciences money is increasingly becoming the spur. The consequences of that change among SuperStar biologists, chemists, and physicists for the stature of the United States remains to be seen.

How can you determine whether a professor is bringing prestige to the university? In the absence of being graced by Nobelity, there are awards of varying importance, positions in scholarly and scientific associations earned by a vote of respect from the members, and, of course, the quality of the bibliography. A verifiable test is a job offer from a prestigious campus. It's an indication that the scholar or scientist has arrived, or is on the way to becoming a name professor in his or her field. But there are stories of how that pistol of promotion can backfire. You will recall the untenured assistant professor who was bucking for a promotion and told his departmental chairperson at Forked River State: "Crestfallen U. wants me as a tenured associate professor," to which the chairperson replied: "I hope you will be happy at Crestfallen." When last heard from, he was working a full load in remedial classes at Spearfish Normal!

Training for Research

An accelerating movement in the corporate world is the periodic training of executives. Executives sharpen their skills in training programs often paid for by their employer. The training and retraining throughout their careers is checked by regular performance evaluations.

In the academy the continual training is in scholarship. Journals accept or reject papers while commercial publishers and university presses measure the value of manuscripts. At conferences colleagues challenge the methodology and conclusions of scholarly papers, if not publicly at a session at least privately in the coffee shop. Once published, the article or book is subjected to reviews in journals by authorities in the field. In this training process, for those who choose to participate, the faculty member grows intellectually in the craft of scholarship by being rigorously examined in the substance and style of his or her contribution to knowledge.

In the art of teaching, however, the faculty member finds no such opportunities for growth. Seldom in graduate school is teaching stressed. When a faculty member begins a teaching career, there is little if any guidance from master teachers or even peers. When senior professors or deans do visit a classroom, it is for evaluative purposes. To videotape a lecture with the intent of improving performance is to invade the sanctity of the classroom. To use student evaluations of teaching in order to improve faculty performance by means of systematic training is to ask the examined to improve the examiners.

Evaluating Administrators

The attitude of business executives and the faculty differ towards their leaders. Business executives are probably not great fans of the top management of their firms, but it is hard to believe they show the same disrespect as faculty do for deans, provosts, and presidents. When asked: "How would you rate the administration at your institution?", and given the choice of excellent, good, fair, and poor, 64% of the faculty said fair or poor. The research and doctorate-granting universities were even more unkind. Over 70% voted fair or poor with 34% of the 70% declaring poor!

Business executives want to be promoted to the jobs of their bosses and may even want to be like them in some way. While some faculty long to be a dean or a president, many do not and do not particularly respect the qualities that such offices require.

Q: What do you have when five administrators are buried up to their neck in sand?

A: Not enough sand.

The administration is basement, not the admired apex of the pyramid. It is where the utilities are stored to service the faculty so they can get on with the primary work of the institution—teaching and research. The administration as a "necessary evil" is a phrase often invoked, but the reproach lacks refinement. There is, let's be fair, nothing *morally* reprehensible about the administration.

In a profound sense, in at least one respect, the faculty are correct—which no doubt helps to contribute to their arrogance about administrators. University presidents do not contribute directly to the colleges' "prestige centers." Scholars do that work. Business CEO's *do* contribute directly to "profit centers." They actively participate in manufacturing, finance, and sales with a daily hands-on involvement in making money. College presidents do not contribute to knowledge through research. Thus do corporate presidents go to the office to be served by vice-presidents; college presidents go to the office to serve the faculty. Businessmen manage; college presidents are more passive—they administer.

5. CURRICULUM—"A BUZZING CONFUSION OF COMPLAINTS"

The product of a university is its course of study or curriculum. A curricular service differs from a business product most strikingly in the absence of quality control. The academic administration of a prestigious university manages its course of study with benign neglect. The more prestigious the institution, the more powerful the faculty, the more benign the neglect.

There are a number of reasons for the lack of quality control over a course of study and the performance of the faculty. First, the creation of courses is largely controlled by departments, not by the central administration. Second, there is very little, if any, evaluation of a professor in the classroom. Third, the principle of academic freedom forbids anyone from interfering in the shaping of the service, especially the ideological cast of the course. Fourth, professors are tenured for life, not for proficiency in offering the curricular service, but for potential in publishing the results of their research.

The lack of quality control is compounded by forces that deflect the managerial energies of the university president from the internal affairs of the campus. A university's reputation is not made by superior undergraduate teaching. It is established by a steady flow of money from government, corporations, alumni, and foundations. A productive faculty converts the money into knowledge, hopes for a favorable evaluation by its peers, and returns to patrons for further sustenance.

University presidents are easily seduced into believing that their universities, under *their* leadership, are compelled to rise to the challenge of solving, not messy campus issues, but the problems of the nation itself. It's rather like the President of the United States finding foreign affairs especially glamorous. How can wrangling with congressional leaders about guns compare to conferring with other heads-of-state about atomic bombs? It's sort of like the husband who explained that his wife made the insignificant decisions, such as what kind of house to buy, where to spend their vacations, and who would be their friends while he made the really

39

important decisions—how to reduce the trade deficit and solve the problems of the Middle East.

The university's role *off-campus* was emphasized in 1991 by the retiring president of Harvard. After twenty years it was time for summing up as Derek Bok delivered his last commencement address as president. He brushed aside the issues that were dominating news stories about higher education in the early 1990's. "There is a buzzing confusion of complaints," he grumbled, "over tuition, over financial aid practices, over reading lists, over affirmative action, even over modern literary theory. And though these are all legitimate issues, the fact that they should dominate the debate about American higher education only shows how muddled we have become about why universities truly matter to society." The social responsibilities of higher education, Bok declared, are to provide education for "humane citizenship" and to help solve the nation's problems. He emphasized a pressing responsibility to focus campus research on off-campus problems. "Research on school reform, on poverty, on crime, on many other social afflictions lags far behind the urgency of these problems for our society. Surely, these shortcomings make a more important subject for debate than most of the issues that have dominated recent discussions about higher education."

Even a retiring president of Harvard can be wrong. No subjects about higher education are more open to debate than what it costs to go to college ("tuition"), how to pay for it ("financial aid practices"), what to study ("reading lists"), who shall attend ("affirmative action"), and how courses should be taught ("modern literary theory".) (He failed to include the complaint of "unsatisfactory undergraduate teaching.") Most university presidents would not dare dismiss such issues as "a buzzing confusion of complaints"—even though the sanctuary of retirement might tempt them to do so. Most doubtless do take the complaints very seriously. However, spending time on solving campus problems means less energy for expanding the reputation of the university as a major player in the affairs of the nation.

Telling Ourselves Who We Are

Why has the press recently tuned into and begun to report on this "buzzing confusion of complaints?" From cover stories to talk shows, the curricular battles on campuses across the nation had become news. The dissension was timely, unusual, and controversial; it was also significant news. The curriculum, counsels historian Frederick Rudolph, "has been

The purpose of both chapters is twofold. One purpose is to reveal the kinds of problems that confront a university in delivering its primary service to the student consumer. A course of study is, by its nature, ideological. The humanities, for example, ask not "Will it sell," as a business must, but "Is it any good?" Even the natural sciences convey a value judgment by selecting one subject rather than another for a laboratory experiment. The product is inevitably controversial. Something of that ideological turbulence is revealed here.

The other purpose is to affirm that a university campus is not an ideological ivory tower. It may indeed be an ivory tower of impractical *means* sheltering professors who never met a payroll, but it should, and often does, engage daily the most worldly of *ends*. Classroom battles spill into the community to become policy issues. Strains in campus living mirror behavioral conflicts which also abuse the nation in offices, factories, and neighborhoods.

Readers interested in a more rounded view of university culture should continue reading this and the next chapter on curriculum. *Readers interested only in the doable reforms should skip to Chapter 7 on students as consumers.* The content of the university product is untouchable. It is the unhappy price that must be paid for academic freedom. Even the administration is virtually powerless. It can cut a department's budget; it can't tell the department what to teach or the spin to put on the subject matter. The college classroom is sacred territory, dependent on the responsible behavior of the teacher. In the other chapters of this study the queries leading to reforms can force a faculty to do a better job of teaching at less cost. The objective throughout is not to control the interpretation of what is taught, but to control the costs of teaching and to improve the quality of delivery. This chapter and the next are about curricular brawls of interpretation defined by selection and emphasis.

* * *

How should subjects be taught? For *cultural conservatives*, the principles were clear:

1) There is no single cause that determines how the world works.

2) A work of literature may explore a variety of human concerns. Paramount is how a novel, poem, or play expresses beauty—the aesthetics of its form, content, and style. Works of literature, as well as paintings, architecture, and music, are not generally, and most certainly not inexorably, political statements.

3) There are absolutes that can be established against criteria of desirability, e.g., if the good of the people is a high priority, then a democracy of laws is a better form of government to strive towards than a dictatorship of the ruler.

4) Standards should be established that set goals and define measurements for their achievement.

5) The text, whether it be a novel, play, or poem, speaks with an inherent meaning and is not dependent upon external circumstances.

6) The forms that writers use to express meaning are not equal. An epic poem is superior to a comic strip.

7) The work of art is superior to its critic.

The *revisionists* were shocking in their defiance. (To make comparisons easier, similar points made by both cultural conservatives and revisionists carry *the same numbers*.):

1) The university mirrors society. The world is divided into the oppressors and the oppressed. The driving force is the conflict between the exploiters and the exploited. In that conflict the victims in the university are blacks, Hispanics, Native-Americans, homosexuals, and women.

2) Works of literature, as well as paintings, architecture, and music, are political and should be viewed as instruments of either oppression or liberation. The humanities can correctly be taught as a conspiracy of propaganda to defend authority. Political content is the most important thing about everything.

3) Value judgments are relative to the culture. They have meaning only within the context of their society. Values are wrongly assumed to be right as a matter of principle. Absolutes asserted as superior values, e.g., democracy's respect for the will of the people, or that government should be obedient to laws rather than to the emotions of the ruler, are neither superior nor inferior ways of governing but valid only for the culture that professes them.

4) Standards preserve the supremacy of those who consider themselves supreme. An appeal to 'quality' is an exclusionary tool of the culturally powerful. The attention to the form of a work of art rather than the artist's message is a submission to European aesthetics. A disregard of the artist's race and gender prejudices correct evaluations.

5) The meaning of a text, e.g., a novel, is not in what the story says, or even the intent of the author, but in the response of the reader. Meaning is in the head of the reader, not the body of the text. A work of art is what each individual critic says it is.

6) All forms of textual expression are equal. One is not superior to another.

7) The critic is equal, maybe even superior, to the novelist, poet, painter, or composer. The critic is a producer of meanings.

* * *

What should be taught? For cultural conservatives, the principles were obvious:

8) Western civilization is the heritage of American society. That heritage begins with ancient Greece and Rome and the Judaic-Christian tradition. It began with the ancients 2,500 years ago and evolved through the Middle Ages, the Renaissance, and the Reformation to the Enlightenment. The values of that civilization, interacting with new world conditions, shaped the American experience. To know who we are, and what we are striving to be, we must first understand that heritage and its transformation into the United States of America.

9) A canon of great works has earned its preeminence over the centuries. Western civilization is its source. The canon is not fixed but responds to the concerns of a period. While works are added and others moved to a secondary rank, the core is sustained. The classics stand the test of time—the kind of books that stick to your ribs. They endure from one generation to the next because they speak meaningfully to the human condition. Americans should treasure the good fortune that much of the literature they read is written in the language they speak—the literature over the centuries of England, Scotland, Ireland, and Wales with additions from British colonies.

10) What should be studied and evaluated is "the best which has been thought and said. . . ," in the words of Matthew Arnold.

The revisionists were contemptuous in their demands for change:

8) For Afrocentrism, Egypt was the womb of Western civilization, and ancient Egyptians were predominantly black. The Greeks stole this heritage of Western civilization and made it their own. Afrocentrism teaches that blacks should be deeply proud of the contribution of their African forebears to what the Greeks claimed to be their own.

45

9) For revisionists in general, the traditional canon is enslaved by a Eurocentrist bias for the works of dead, white, European males (DWEMS.) The dominance of thinkers and writers like Plato, Aristotle, Shakespeare, and T. S. Eliot discriminates against Third World contributions. The canon is impoverished by its disregard of ethnic diversity.

10) Who decides what is "the best which has been thought and said?" What does "best" mean? What is "best" is decided by the academic power structure which defines best as that which is most like itself.

* * *

Why teach it? For cultural conservatives, certain principles were worth reaffirmation:

11) The incontestable objective of a course of study is the pursuit of truth. The goal is not what to think, but what to think *about*. The way to truth is through the use of reason. People of good will recognize their frailty in succumbing to subjective biases. Teachers and students (scholars, too) are not disinterested in the subject studied nor detached from it. Still, slippery truth *can* be pursued with objective intent, however imperfect the truth revealed, however stained the intent with subjectivity. Cultural conditioning may influence our judgment; it need not determine it.

12) America is *e pluribus unum*. Out of many nationalities, one nation has been created. Ethnic loyalties now tear apart nations around the globe. Americans should be taught to appreciate their shared values. The assimilation of immigrants into a national identity is a tradition as old as George Washington's declaration in 1794. Washington questioned the advisability of immigrants coming over and settling as a group. "By so doing, they retain the Language, habits and principles (good or bad) which they bring with them," he wrote to John Adams. "Whereas by an intermixture with our people, they, or their descendants, get assimilated to our customs, measures and laws: in a word, soon become one people." Respect can and should be accorded to the achievements of *pluribus* but not by a fragmenting tribalism. *Unum* is the glue of ideals within a shared experience that binds together to a common cause 250,000,000 people across a continent of 3,000 miles.

13) Rights reside in the individual. Individuals increasingly do, and indeed should, take their sense of identity from the achieved

accomplishments of the self rather than the ascribed determinants of race, ethnicity, class, region, or religion.

Revisionists mounted nothing less than a Heimlich Maneuver on what they saw as a body academic choking on its own bone of errors:

11) The objective of a course of study depends on the person doing the teaching. Teachers, students, and scholars are so deterministically culture-bound that they cannot transcend their prejudices to seek something so elusive as the truth. Even to attempt impartiality is an impossibility.

12) The contributions of racial and ethnic groups to the mosaic of American life have been ignored. Multiculturalism argues that the rich texture of the nation should not only be acknowledged in the past but maintained in the present. The "melting pot" is a degrading metaphor. Ethnic and racial groups should glory in their differentness and organize ways to preserve it.

Assimilation can be tyranny. The psyches of young Afro-Americans, Latino-Americans, Asian-Americans, and Native-Americans have been wounded by a curricular prejudice. Self-esteem will rise when their suffering is acknowledged, their differentness recognized, their contributions identified, and their heritage restored.

13) America is a sexist, racist society oppressing women and people of color. The oppressed can find strength only in the group. Individualism undermines group solidarity in the group's quest for social justice. Individualism benefits individuals who control power. Accentuating gender and race resists the tyranny of assimilation and supports the liberation of the group.

* * *

Who should teach? Cultural conservatives emphasized proven merit and credentials:

14) Properly trained teachers transcend the subject taught. Teachers are not required to experience personally the subjects they are teaching. A white teacher can help students understand a novel about black inner city life even though the teacher has never experienced living in an inner city. It is not required to ship aboard a whaling vessel to interpret *Moby Dick*.

Revisionists advanced another criterion:

14) Who teaches affects in predestined ways what is taught. Authenticity lives within the skin of the interpreter. You can

47

only teach what you are. Role models should be selected from the race and gender of the oppressed.

* * *

Who should be taught?

15) On admissions policies, cultural conservatives split into the more familiar dichotomy of political conservatives and political liberals. The political conservatives argued that race should not be a selective factor for admission to college. Preference and aid should be awarded on the basis of economic class. If affirmative action was shifted from race to class, whites would no longer resent reverse discrimination. Class-based affirmative action would still overwhelmingly benefit blacks who disproportionately number among the poor. Affirmative action based on race gives an unfair advantage to the children of an increasingly numerous black middle class. Affirmative action was never meant to be a permanent but only a transition program. The transition is over.

15) Revisionists, joined by most political liberals, argued that preferential treatment for admissions should be based on race (including Hispanics) as well as economic class. Blacks and other racial groups should be compensated for past and existing injustices, especially the exclusion from educational and job opportunities.

Political Correctness in Historical Perspective

How deeply have the revisionists penetrated the curriculum? Do the disagreements really make any difference for the destiny of the Republic? The writer Joseph Epstein wasn't prepared to get too cosmic about it, but he knew who the true victims were: "Harvard, Yale, Princeton, Stanford and other only scarcely less august institutions compete among themselves lest they be caught without a goodly supply of angry teachers of victimological subjects. Irony of ironies, nuttiness of nuttiness, the scene thus presented is that of the fortunate teaching the privileged that the world is by and large divided between the oppressed and the oppressors, victims and executioners, and that the former are inevitably morally superior. As a tuition-paying parent, I used sometimes to think, writing out those heavy checks to universities, that the only true victims in this entire arrangement were those of us who helped to pay for it all."

Epstein was correct about the irony. The radical credo has penetrated more deeply into the prestigious universities and liberal arts colleges. Less vociferous were the faculty of institutions with modest pretensions, especially faculty in the municipal community colleges where genuine Third World immigrants were grabbing for bootstraps. The daily exertion there was to get out of being a victim, not relish its ideological comforts. To be born a victim may be bad but to die like one was worse.

Many campuses went untouched or easily absorbed radical challenges to the curriculum. However, at some eminent universities quarreling over the course of study split open the faculty like an axe. At others faculty were intimidated for failing to express what came to be known as "politically correct" viewpoints. Teachers and students accused of injuring the sensitivities of blacks, gays, or women were said to be harshly used. There was a growing feeling of unease, especially at large universities with an ethnically diversified student body living in residential campuses. The risk was in the word, not the deed. "There really is a lot of anxiety now surfacing over the term 'diversity,'" Jason McIntosh, a student senator at the University of Kansas explained in 1991. "People are so afraid to say anything because they don't want to be called racists. Nobody has given us a road map."

The censorial extent of political correctness to enforce conformity is difficult to measure, but the President of the United States felt compelled to call attention to it. "The notion of political correctness has ignited controversy across the land," George Bush declared at the University of Michigan's 1991 commencement. "And although the movement arises from the laudable desire to sweep away the debris of racism and sexism and hatred, it replaces old prejudice with new ones. It declares certain topics off-limits, certain expression off-limits, even certain gestures off-limits. What began as a crusade for civility has soured into a cause of conflict and even censorship. Disputants treat sheer force—getting their foes punished or expelled, for instance—as a substitute for the power of ideas."

The unhappy experience of Harvard University's Stephan Thernstrom became one of the more publicized cases of political correctness (PC) in the late 1980s. Thernstrom was a respected scholar of ethnicity. He was charged with making statements in his course offensive to the feelings of black students. It was a nasty proceeding, especially for Thernstrom who reported that he was "absolutely stunned" by the complaint of racism. The comments the students "attributed to me were a ridiculous distortion of what I said in class." Thernstrom confided that

49

"it's like being called a Commie in the fifties. Whatever explanation you offer, once accused, you're always suspect." The Harvard professor could not resist a wry observation: "In classes at elite campuses you still can freely take pot shots at Mormons, Texans, the Marine Corps, right-to-lifers, fraternity and sorority members, and, indeed, Republicans. But watch what you say about 'oppressed groups.'"

So what else is new? The liberal arts faculties of eminent universities, at least for the last half century, have generally sympathized with oppressed groups. What's changed is who is designated as oppressed. At prestigious universities the faculties (much to the distress of many alumni) predominantly have been politically liberal and registered to vote as Democrats. The liberal tilt has been more pronounced in the social sciences and humanities than in the natural sciences. A recent survey in 1989 disclosed that 67% of the faculty of research universities characterized themselves politically as liberals while 17% confessed to being conservative. For all higher educational institutions, 70% in the humanities characterized themselves as liberals with 18% conservatives. In the social sciences 70% said they were liberals and 15% conservatives. The rest acknowledged to being middle-of-the-road.

Within the predominantly liberal cast of the faculties of research universities there have always been left-leaning extremists. The *authority* condemned as oppressive a half century ago by the radicals was the economic force of capitalism. An oppressed *group* was the proletariatian wage earner. Currently, the *authority* that is viewed as oppressive is the cultural force of Eurocentrism, assimilationism, the canon of great works, and Dead White European Males. Currently oppressed *groups* are blacks, Native-Americans, gays, and women. A half century ago an unkind view was that a left-leaning love of the poor was masquerading as a hatred of plutocracy. Today, it's a love of multicultural diversity disguised as a contempt for meritocracy. The constant is the attack on authority; the variable is the definition of authority.

"Who Controls the Past Controls the Future."

The academic brawl over the curriculum was elevated to newsworthy prominence in the late 1980s and early 1990s. The press recognized that professors and students were not squabbling in an ivory tower aloof from practical affairs. The argument was going to have consequences for the kind of society America intended to be. How students view the past shapes the nation's future. "Who controls the past controls the future,"

50

proclaims the frightening slogan in George Orwell's *Nineteen Eighty-Four*. "Who controls the present controls the past."

It was the role of race, both how it should be interpreted in the past and confronted in the present, which was surfacing across the nation on college campuses. One reason is revealed in the statistics. In 1980 one out of five people in the United States was black, Hispanic, Asian, or American Indian. By 1990 the ratio was one in four. During the 1980s the black population grew by 13%, the Hispanic population by 53%, Asians by 107%, and American Indians by 38%. The white population grew by 6%.

Universities were forced to respond to the troubling issue of race, not only as an ideological issue but because more minorities were enrolling each year. Within this changing student population, several forces began colliding with each other on college campuses during the 1980s. One force was the emergence of a strong tolerance ethic of racial equality. It was wrong in the most profound *moral* sense to discriminate on the basis of race. Racism, confirmed the President of the United States in 1991, was "an intolerable sin." In a Judaic-Christian society, to sin in thought, word, or deed—and to be made aware of it—is to feel guilt.

Another force was affirmative action. Race was becoming an approved identifier as the nation became more racially diversified. The payoff of affirmative action granted preferential treatment to minorities. The collision was the growing feeling that affirmative action was a form of reverse discrimination against whites, that preferential treatment based on race was a repudiation of the tolerance ethic of equality.

The irony is that affirmative action laws accentuated racial identification, presumably for the purpose of erasing that identification. The irony was deepened by professional ethnics who were hired to reduce race as a source of conflict. Their importance expanded, their salaries rose, and their numbers swelled in the degree to which race surfaced in the news as a problem.

To this uneasy mix was added another force that was an unintended consequence of affirmative action. Blacks were not always certain whether their admission to the university (or to law or medical school) was racial preference or academic merit. The uncertainty undermined self-esteem. Young blacks, unable to satisfy a need for self-respect in the heritage of slavery, began searching for self-esteem in African roots.

Most other ethnic groups, with the exception of those Hispanics who were advocating bilingual education as an instrument for maintaining loyalty to Latino ways, had been loosening their ties to the "old country." To be sure, there were the annual weekend get-togethers of ethnic food, colorful costumes, and folk dancing. If there were enough Poles or Italians or Irish or Hungarians or Lithuanians around, and someone was energetic enough to do the organizing, there might even be a parade led by the mayor who on that always sunny day was miraculously converted into one of their own. The next day it was back to the shopping mall. Most ethnic festivities glowed with the coziness of nostalgia, not the demanding clamor of an ideology.

For blacks a far deeper sense of the ego was involved. Geography for some was becoming more important than color. Many blacks began to emphasize their hyphenation as African-Americans. The irony, of course, is that blacks had been natives of America far longer than most nineteenth century immigrant groups. No matter. The textbook, *Lessons from History: A Celebration in Blackness* explained: "Mexicans are called Mexicans because there is a land named Mexico. Now look at the map. Is there a place called Colorland? Negroland? Blackland? No. There is a land named Africa, which is where we came from. So, in our book, we shall refer to ourselves as Africans, African-Americans, and Africans in America." When students asked why the Great Sphinx at Giza in Egypt had no nose, they were taught that "Napoleon was so jealous of this great feat he ordered twenty-one shells of fire aimed at the face of the Sphinx to alter its facial features so people would not know it was African. Despite the damage from this 'twenty-one gun salute,' the Sphinx is still recognizably African."

Egyptians were really Africans. One of the reasons why we know that, explained Professor Asa G. Hilliard of Georgia State University, is that the Greek historian Herodotus described the people he saw in Egypt as "'burnt skinned, flat nosed, thick lipped, and wooly haired.'" Since it was the Egyptians, not the thieving Greeks, who were the true founders of Western civilization, and since the Egyptians were black Africans, Africa was the womb of what is now celebrated as Greek in origin. In *Stolen Legacy*, professor George G. M. James, a leading historian of Afrocentrism, confessed that he was "happy to be able to bring this information to the attention of the world, so that on the one hand, all races and creeds might know the truth and free themselves from those prejudices which have corrupted human relations; and on the other hand, that the people of African origin might be emancipated from their serfdom of [an] inferiority complex, and enter upon a new era of freedom in which they would feel like free men, with full human rights and privileges."

No one quarreled with the objectives of reducing prejudice and increasing Afro-American self-esteem. Respected Egyptologists were upset by the way it was being done. "The concept of pharaonic Egypt as a high civilization created by black Africans is profoundly disturbing to almost every scholar outside the black community, as well as to some within that community. . . ," growled ancient historian James Muhly. "The claims being made for African Egypt as the originator of all the arts of civilization are gross distortions of reality and, at their worst, represent a cruel hoax being foisted on black people in America."

Professor Muhly was surprised during a 1990 symposium at Philadelphia's Temple University about "the depth of interest in and dedication to the Black Egypt concept on the part of the blacks at the symposium, those on the program as well as those in the audience." Journalists were reporting that Afrocentrism, rather than being shot down trailing smoke into the wreckage of disproved interpretations, was soaring into the inner city public schools of major cities. The whole thing was getting uncomfortable for whites. Should one ask a black colleague at the office what tribe he belonged to?

"White Guilt Can Be Pushed Too Far."

The clash of morality in the tolerance ethic, legality in affirmative action, and uneasiness about Afrocentric courses set off confrontational sparks. The journalist-commentator Samuel Francis was harsh: "One of the hidden purposes of Afrocentrism as an ideology, and of the whole racism racket by which traditional values are challenged as racially biased, is to concoct justifications for the lackluster performance of blacks in the United States." Educational analyst Diane Ravitch advised that "it is dangerous to turn history into a feel-good course. . . . It may be impossible to teach the participation of Africans and Arabs in the slave trade, because their descendents find such references objectionable. . . . The only villains in the history-for-self-esteem movement . . . are white males, because they are not an oppressed minority."

Another unintended consequence of preferential treatment in college admissions and scholarships, surrounded by assertions of black pride, was white resentment. The grumbling about a double standard was beginning to be heard in the high schools. A 16-year old complained that blacks "wear those T-shirts that say, 'It's a black thing. You wouldn't understand.' If we did that, we'd be called racists. If they do it, it's their right."

Resentment about a double standard that favors blacks to the disadvantage of whites was beginning to dissolve white guilt. It was the feeling of white guilt, activated by conscience, that empowered the black-initiated civil rights movement. Any weakening of that guilt would alter profoundly race relations on American campuses. Andrew Milot, a recent senior at the University of Michigan, described himself as a political liberal. "There has been a lingering guilt with me for a long time," he confessed. He felt partly responsible for the historical crimes of slavery, segregation, and subjugation. "But now I feel like *I'm* the one under attack. To some extent, I have lost my old guilt." Indeed, Arthur M. Schlesinger, Jr., the quintessential intellectual of political liberalism, could be brought to such a point in his life of actions and passions to protest the trashing of Western civilization's record on human rights and cry out in protesting prophecy: "White guilt can be pushed too far."

What Kind of a Place Should America Be?

Innovations in college curriculums sometimes herald public policy issues. Arguments about spins on the course of study are later played out in the halls of legislatures and courts of law. What should be public policy on immigration, affirmative action, set-asides for minorities, bi-lingual education, proportional representation based on race, gender-specific regulations?

The old arguments about curricular spin were about the role of politics in economic affairs. How much income should be transferred from the richer to the poorer for a more just society? How much should the government regulate business for the common good? The new arguments are about race, ethnicity, and gender. What role should they play in the kind of place America should be? That question has been asked throughout the nation's history but never with the same forceful articulation.

The American story has been the assimilation of ethnic and racial diversity into an American ethos. Shall that assimilationist persuasiveness be sustained in the schools and colleges, or shall ethnic and racial differences be accentuated in the next century for a different kind of country? Thomas Sobel, the powerful Education Commissioner of New York State, agreed with the multiculturalists. "Mr. Sobel, the son of a boxcar loader," Joseph Berger reported, "conceded that he had managed to be successful without learning much about his father's Polish roots. But he said the world has changed. The diversity of America's population is no longer purely European in origin, and *ethnic consciousness has replaced assimilation as the American ethic.*"

Thus, it is the Hispanic writer who is prized rather than the writer who happens to be Hispanic. The significant characteristic of Hawthorne and Melville is that they are white and male just as Edith Wharton and Willa Cather are white and female. Abraham Lincoln, with his zeal for self-education, is not a role model for all but for whites only. Martin Luther King, Jr., in his passion for racial justice, is an archetype for blacks only.

The University of California at Berkeley is currently phasing in a required course for graduation. The student selects from a list of approved courses. Each course must compare at least three of five ethnic groups—"African Americans, Asian Americans, Chicano/Latino Americans, and American Indians." There are no Americans. The fifth ethnic group is "European Americans."

6. CURRICULUM—MULTICULTURALISM

"Hey, hey, ho, ho. Western culture has got to go," chanted the marching Stanford University students. Alarmists across the nation read about the widely reported 1987 incident and predicted the fall of American civilization. The omnipresent Jesse Jackson, of course, was there. Had the rainbow coalition regrouped to persuade, not voters at the ballot box, but students in the classroom?

One suspects that the rejecting chant was a student caper of mocking defiance. As it turned out, Jesse Jackson advised against jettisoning Western culture but called rather for embracing the contributions of other cultures. The demonstration concluded with Jackson leading the 500 protesters in "We Shall Overcome." Sure, the vision of a Stanford University undergraduate struggling against oppression *is* hard to bring into focus. No problem, as the saying of calming reassurance goes. The Stanford faculty was on the way to approving required courses that not only stressed cross-cultural comparisons with Western civilization but especially emphasized the non-European contributions of minorities and women to American culture.

There are victors in curricular battles, and there are losers. Scholars of considerable eminence were choosing up sides, not only to debate the course of study, but to chart a course for the nation. Harvard University's Henry Louis Gates, Jr., an African-American, represented one view: "What has passed as 'common culture' has been an Anglo-American regional culture, masking itself as universal. . . . To demand that Americans shuck their cultural [i.e., ethnic] heritages and homogenize themselves into a 'universal' WASP culture is to dream of an America in cultural white face, and that just won't do. . . . The challenge facing America will be the shaping of a truly common public culture, one responsive to the long-silenced cultures of color. If we relinquish the ideal of America as a plural nation, we've abandoned the very experiment America represents."

Yale University's Dean Donald Kagan advised his entering freshmen to chart a different course: "Americans do not share a common ancestry and a common blood. What they have in common is a system of laws and beliefs that shaped the establishment of the country, a system developed within the context of Western civilization. . . . Happily, student bodies have grown vastly more diverse. Less happily, students see themselves increasingly as parts of groups, distinct from other groups. . . . Take pride in your family and in the culture they and your forebears have brought to our shores. Learn as much as you can about that culture. Learn as much as you can of what the particular cultures of others have to offer. But do not fail to learn the great traditions that are the special gifts of Western civilization."

What particularly bothered the cultural conservatives was the projection of Western radical and feminist views onto third-world cultures. "American universities typically teach non-Western courses in a manner bearing little or no resemblance to the ideas most deeply cherished in those cultures," argued Dinesh D'Souza, a leading traditionalist. "Instead, most American students receive a selective polemical interpretation of non-Western societies, one that reveals less about those places than about the ideological prejudices of those who manage multicultural education. . . . Authentic multicultural education would challenge the materialism of American students by exposing them to the spiritual claims of the East. It would teach the future leaders of this country something about the roots of East Asian capitalism and Islamic fundamentalism—two forces with which American business and culture will have to contend."

The cultural conservatives admitted that there was an uncomfortable gap between the ideals of Western civilization and their reality, between the rhetoric of preachment and the brute practice. But they clung to those shared ideas and revered values, modified by the American experience, that had held the nation together and given it direction.

Some cultural conservatives argued in terms of Western civilization's advantages while others focused more exclusively on the American expression of those values. A few were more rancorous than perhaps necessary. Historian Forrest McDonald no doubt meant to be instructive: "Though advocates of abandoning the study of Western Civ do not realize it, one of the primary values of studying non-Western cultures is that it teaches us how vastly superior the West is and how limiting and debasing are its alternatives."

Western civilization, its defenders explained, either initiated or established what the people of Africa, the Middle East, and Asia hunger for. What Western civilization offers is models of democracy with an accountable executive, freely elected legislatures, an independent judiciary, the rule of law, and the kind of human rights specified in the Bill of Rights of the United States Constitution—notably freedom of speech, press, and religion. West is not necessarily best, but from Western civilization flow the values that guided nations to a democratic way of governing, a capitalistic way of producing, and a scientific way of thinking.

Foreign to the West in modern times are such practices as a caste system and the subjugation of women by forced marriages, clitoridectomy, foot-binding, and wife-burning upon the husband's death. Indeed, the ancient and universal practice of slavery was abolished, not by African and Asian societies that cooperated in the selling into slavery of their peoples, but by the Christian conscience of the West.

Particularly frightening to cultural conservatives was multiculturalism striking so near to the heartbeat of a central doctrine in the American credo. What does it mean to be an American? What does it mean to be a Korean? Well, for one thing, a Korean *looks* like a Korean. An American can look like *anybody*. The Japanese or the French are exclusionary cultures. They are not comfortable with people who don't look and talk like what they think a Japanese or French person should look and talk like. They don't adopt strangers the way America has since its inclusionary beginning. *Anyone* can become an American. Since anyone from some other country can become what people here already are, both old-timers as well as newcomers must keep defining what an American is and what the United States stands for. You have to keep testifying to a faith in shared ideals. That's why such a simple ritual as the Pledge of Allegiance is essential. Like a religious disciple regularly professing to a credo with the same words, American children pledge allegiance to the belief that all may have liberty and justice. In a nation of immigrants, it's a way of making certain the succeeding generation remembers what the departing generation has tried to live for, and, of course, failed to live up to.

Cultural conservatives agreed with the multiculturalists that the study of ethnic and racial diversity should be incorporated into the curriculum. They cautioned against attributing to that diversity a greater significance in American society than the evidence revealed. They protested against the debasing of Western civilization. They became alarmed when diversity was brandished as a divisive instrument contributing to ethnic and racial discord. They warned that the ties that bind countries into a national community are fragile.

California introduced a multicultural curriculum into the public schools. It was criticized by numerous ethnic representatives. Bill Honig, the California state superintendent with a reputation as a political liberal, struck at the "victimization crew . . . tribalists . . . separatists [in universities who] make a livelihood on discrediting broader cultural ideas. . . . They do not like the idea of common democratic principles. It gets in the way of their left point of view that this country is corrupt. This country has been able to celebrate pluralism but keep some sense of the collective that holds us together. Everything is not race, gender or class. The whole world cannot be seen just through those glasses. . . . If everything becomes hostile race and class warfare, we are going to lose this country. The issue is not multiculturalism. We agree with that. The question is, Are you also going to talk about the political and moral values that are essential for us to live together?"

For better or worse, the womb of those values was Great Britain. Anglo-Saxon Protestant codes of behavior and values were the tradition to which immigrants were expected to conform. The mechanisms of assimilation ranged from a free public school system to the necessity of learning a common language. The unifying force of that common language was threatened by a linguistic expression of multiculturalism—bilingualism when used to sustain a competing language. E. D. Hirsch, Jr. in his influential *Cultural Literacy: What Every American Needs to Know* warned that "it is contrary to the purpose and essence of a national language . . . that a modern nation should deliberately encourage more than one to flourish within its borders. . . . When two great standard literate languages like English and Spanish . . . coexist inside a nation, neither can yield to the other except by strife or vigorous intervention in the educational system. . . . Defenders of multilingualism should not assume that our Union has been preserved once and for all by the Civil War. . . ."

Who Am I? Who Are You?

At the center of the discord was a principle of profound meaning for the American ethos—how was an American to represent one's self? Was it as a member of a group? Are we primarily members of a race, ethnic

60

clan, family, church, region, political party? Or are we first of all individuals?

The majority of people in the world identify themselves by their family in an hierarchical society of ascribed status. In America, a person takes his or her sense of identity from the self as an individual. That trend has accelerated in recent decades. Most prominent is the sundering of gender and role. Wife-mother, like husband-father, has broken the tyranny of gender over role and is offered the option of a breadwinning career.

Multiculturalism is a countervailing force to the trend that defines the identity of the individual by the self. Instead of emphasizing the unique specialness of the individual regardless of gender, family, or or even physical disability, multiculturalists stressed the ascribed characteristic of race and ethnicity. The initiative was particularly emphatic in the writing of books for children. "If black children or Native Americans or Asians don't see themselves in books," argued Professor Roberta Long, who teaches a course in children's literature, "they won't see themselves as important people. And we will be sending that message to white children, too." The "see themselves" mandate for the school curriculum was reaffirmed by Marcy C. Canavan, a school board member in Maryland: "I and most white Americans know about our history. We learn about the Pilgrims. All our students should be able to hear about their ancestors."

To view the Pilgrims as "our history," white history, jolted a comfortable faith in a common culture. The common culture of the United States transcended ethnicity or race to invoke symbols of a common faith—the Pilgrims at a thanksgiving dinner expressing gratitude for the blessings of the New World; Benjamin Franklin disciplining us that early to bed and early to rise makes a man healthy, wealthy, and wise; Thomas Jefferson proclaiming that we have inalienable rights; the Founding Fathers shaping the Constitution that hot summer in Philadephia; Abraham Lincoln at Gettysburg defining for us a democracy and pledging that governments of the people, by the people, and for the people shall endure; and on and on to Martin Luther King, Jr.'s dream that we be judged, not by the color of our skin, but by the content of our character.

Multiculturalists contended that blacks would find their self-esteem in Martin Luther King, Jr., not Abraham Lincoln. (Whether whites would naturally find greater self-esteem in Lincoln than in King was not so often pondered.) Self-esteem was seen to be increasingly dependent on the particularism of color and eye shape. It was to the individual as a

61

member of a group, rather than the individual as a universal symbol for all, to whom minorities should turn for emulative models. Basketball player Michael Jordan was attacked by baseball's Hank Aaron and football's Jim Brown, all professional superstars and all black, for not speaking out more visibly in black communities. "I think that kind of criticism is totally unfair," countered Jordan. "I've been trying to have people view me more as a good person than a good black man. I know I'm black. I was born black and I'll die black. . . . Because I want every kid to be viewed as a person rather than as a member of a certain race does not mean I'm not black enough."

Who am I? Who are you? The questions are ancient; each age answers them in response to principal concerns. On American campuses across the nation in the 1980s committees were meeting to confront those questions. An exchange of correspondence in 1989 between two members of a diversity committee at the University of Pennsylvania addressed the issue of the individual versus the group with striking clarity. One undergraduate member of the committee that was planning guidelines for residential diversity programs complained that "the desire of the committee to continually consider the collective before the individual is misconceived. At Penn we should be concerned with the intellect and experience of INDIVIDUALS before we are concerned with the group." A university administrator serving on the committee circled the word "INDIVIDUALS" and replied: "This is a 'RED FLAG' phrase today, which is considered by many to be RACIST. Arguments that champion the individual over the group ultimately privileges [sic] the 'individuals' belonging to the largest or dominant group. . . . In a pluralistic society, individuals are only as significant as their group."

Answering the existential question "Who am I?" with an emphasis on group differences had reached the point of alarm for Shelby Steele, a professor of English at California's San Jose State University. "Once every six months or so someone yells 'nigger' at me from a passing car," Steele reported. He didn't care to dwell on the thought that "this chorus might one day soon sing to me from the paths of my own campus." Steele had become a political theorist: "What has emerged on campus in recent years—as a result of the new equality and of affirmative action and, in a sense, as a result of progress—is a *politics of difference*, a troubling, volatile politics in which each group justifies itself, its sense of worth and its pursuit of power, through difference alone. In this context, racial, ethnic, and gender differences become forms of sovereignty, campuses become balkanized, and each group fights with whatever means are available."

Steele continued, reminiscent of the *Federalist Papers* Number 10. In that 1787 communication to the colonies pleading for the ratification of the Constitution, James Madison stated that the primary cause of differences was "the unequal distribution of property." Instead of Madison's economic interpretation based on money, land, and possessions, Steele substituted a multicultural interpretation more relevant for his own time: "Race is, by any standard, an unprincipled source of power. And on campuses the use of racial power by one group makes racial, ethnic, or gender difference a currency of power for all groups. When I make my *difference* into power, other groups must seize upon their difference to contain my power and maintain their position relative to me. Very quickly a kind of politics of difference emerges in which racial, ethnic, and gender groups are forced to assert their entitlement and vie for power based on the single quality that makes them different from one another."

The politics of difference, explained Steele, is reinforced by departments and programs in black studies, women's studies, and Asian studies that offer courses that could just as well be studied within traditional departments. The segregation of blacks in Afro houses and counseling programs aggravates separatism. Rejecting the philosophical position of finding "meaning in difference," Steele concluded that "universities should emphasize commonality as a higher value than 'diversity' and 'pluralism'—buzzwords for the politics of difference."

Finding meaning in racial difference originated another consequence that achieving blacks were finding uncomfortable. Admissions offices were drawing up at least two lists for law or medical or business school. One list was the best qualified. The other list, "best-qualified *black*," is what Stephen Carter called it in *Reflections of an Affirmative Action Baby*.

Carter clerked for Supreme Court Justice Thurgood Marshall and went on to become a professor at the Yale Law School. He told how it felt to be the "best black": "The best black syndrome creates in those of us who have benefited from racial preferences a peculiar contradiction. We are told over and over that we are among the best black people in our professions. And in part we are flattered, or should be, because, after all, those who call us the best black lawyers or doctors or investment bankers consider it a compliment. But to professionals who have worked hard to succeed, flattery of this kind carries an unsubtle insult, for we yearn to be called what our achievements often deserve: simply the best—no qualifiers needed! In *this* society, however, we sooner or later must accept that being viewed as the best blacks is part of what has led us to where we are; and we must further accept that to some of our colleagues, black as well as white, we will never be anything else."

"America Does Not Consist of Groups."

All of us are alive to different loyalties in a pluralist society. We are Protestant, Catholic, or Jew; from the East, West, or South; big city or rural; immigrants or native; management or labor; man or woman; black or white. From moment to moment we shift the weight of our loyalties from one special interest group to another. The groups themselves are not unified. In religion, greater differences frequently emerge *within* Protestant denominations than *between* them. In politics, sometimes more intense disagreements break out *within* the Republican and Democratic parties than *between* them. These endless divisions are vital for our democracy because they prevent any one special-interest group from ganging up on another and seizing all the power for itself. The irony is that multiple loyalties unite us as citizens by dividing us into groups.

Multiculturalism in the curriculum and diversity in campus life produced consequences for the nation in foreign affairs and domestic policy. President Woodrow Wilson warned of the dangers of group identification for United States foreign policy. "You cannot become thorough Americans if you think of yourselves in groups," he told a gathering of naturalized citizens in 1915. "America does not consist of groups. A man who thinks of himself as belonging to a particular national group in America has not yet become an American. . . ."

Wilson was concerned about the loyalty of 'hyphenates' dividing America during World War I. Indeed, during World War I the Germans, and in World War II the Japanese, were perceived to be a threat to national security. Today, the dual loyalty of ethnic groups is not perceived to be a threat to national security. Still, adjusting the national interest abroad to ethnic demands at home enormously complicates the exercise of foreign policy.

To get reelected politicians must respond to the ethnic passions of their constituents. It could be the Irish demanding a more forceful posture about northern Ireland, Greeks about Cyprus, Turks about Cyprus, Jews about Israel, Arabs about Israel, Indians about Pakistan,

Pakistanis about Pakistan, Chinese about Taiwan, Taiwanese about Taiwan, and so forth.

As eastern Europe continues to splinter into ethnic enclaves, the consciousness of corresponding enclaves in the United States will magnify in the degree to which they are encouraged to do so. Americans whose ancestors were Croats, Serbs, Hungarians, Ukranians or Georgians, Estonians, Latvians, or Lithuanians will continue to bond in varying degrees to "the old country." But if their ethnicity is encouraged, and the loyalties of other citizens to their own ethnic group is promoted, their emboldened representatives will seek to play a more commanding role in the shaping of foreign policy. How then shall the national interest be defined? Will United States foreign policy, so long shackled to a bipolar competition with communism, be unchained to follow more closely the dual loyalties of American ethnic groups?

America As an Ethnic Meatgrinder

"History is to the nation . . . ," counselled Arthur Schlesinger, Jr., "as memory is to the individual." Introducing the ideology of multiculturalism into the history of the United States was proving to be divisive beyond the campus. It may have been George Bernard Shaw who scolded the press as "unable, seemingly, to discriminate between a bicycle accident and the collapse of civilization." Multiculturalism was not about the collapse but the interpretation of civilization. The press saw the significance in the story and began to cover it as news.

The 500th anniversary of Columbus's arrival was becoming an occasion for Native Americans to humiliate Italian-Americans. Frank Busnardo, the president of the Federation of Italian-American Organizations in Denver, Colorado, explained that "the theme for our parade is that Columbus is a bridge between two worlds—the Old World and the New World. The Italian community has gotten a bad deal out of this. It's supposed to be for all ethnic groups, including the Indians."

Multiculturalism not only lured ethnic groups into conflict with each other. The ideology sometimes lacked the refinement of historical evidence. Columbus's voyage was a discovery (from the viewpoint of Europe), an encounter (from a detached viewpoint), or an invasion (from the aboriginals' perspective). One Native American referred to the time before the mariner's arrival as "the good old days." For the ravaged Arawak tribe in San Salvador that view is incontestable. Still, the values of Columbus had little influence on shaping the character of the United

65

States. It was Latin America that had the misfortune of being colonized by an authoritarian Spanish culture and a dependency-generating Roman Catholicism. The North America of the United States and Canada had the good fortune to be colonized by a more democratic British culture and a literate-encouraging, individual-asserting, wealth-generating Protestantism—if good fortune be measured by political freedom and economic productivity rather than spiritual salvation.

Multiculturalists sometimes found what they were looking for without much evidence to support it. Food proved that America was a mosaic. Food was the alchemy transforming the American melting pot into a salad bowl. It was as if a slice of pizza pie were to inject an emotionally repressed WASP with the *brio magnifico* of an Italian boulevardier, munching on an egg roll inspire irreverent American teenagers to respect their ancestors, devouring bagels and lox with cream cheese awaken listless college students to the exhilaration of ideas, or nibbling sushi convert the faithless American executive into a loyal corporate employee.

Critical discrimination was absent in the standards for accreditation dictated by the Middle States Association of Colleges and Schools. The accrediting body advised colleges and universities that where possible they should introduce a global perspective in order to "emphasize the cultural diversity and interrelatedness of the contemporary world." A recommended course for a general education would "increase awareness of each individual's own cultural heritage as well as that of others." Several other kinds of courses were recommended. There is nothing about students understanding who they are by a study of American culture and its origins in Western civilization.

A course designed to "increase awareness of each individual's own cultural heritage as well as that of others" accentuates differentness. A question seldom asked in such a course is an evaluative one—does the cultural heritage represent the kind of values and behavior that would make a desirable addition to American culture?

America has been an ethnic meatgrinder—except for isolated flocks like the Amish. A meatgrinder is a pitiless metaphor, but euphemisms only confound an issue which is already obfuscated with misleading postures. The relentlessly grinding process of assimilation makes it possible to support generalizations about the homogeneity of American culture—250 million people and 3,000 miles coast to coast—which would be impossible for most nations of Europe. Every immigrant group brings with it a cultural heritage. To interrupt the assimilation by preserving the values of that ethnic heritage should invite an evaluation of whether the values to be introduced into American culture are preferable to the ones already here.

Further, it is not politic to ask the question whether some immigrant groups have contributed more to America than others, e.g., have Russian Jews, per capita, made a greater contribution than Roman Catholic Peruvians, Buddhist Koreans than Moslem Egyptians? It *is* necessary to ask whether immigrant groups should automatically be encouraged to preserve all the values transported with them from their country of origin. If not all, which ones? Specifically, the Hindu tradition demands the subordination of a wife to her husband; the Moslem tradition will not tolerate free speech about religion, namely Allah; Hispanic culture fails to stress the importance of education, which leads to high dropout rates. Since a Hispanic immigrant with proper papers may qualify for the advantages of affirmative action, while an Irish immigrant and most United States citizens may not, it is reasonable not to wish to preserve those values that disadvantage native-born Americans.

A society is defined by what it is willing to die for. Kazuo Ogura, a Japanese official at the Foreign Ministry, spoke to the point in Japan when he explained that the Japanese feel "a vaguely unsettling sensation" when they are asked by Americans to fight and die for such concepts as "freedom, democracy and the market economy." These values, he said, have no Japanese roots and feel like "a new suit of Western clothes" to most Japanese.

A Fellowship of Shared Ideas

Alexis de Tocqueville, newly arrived in the United States from France in 1831, wrote home that he was "dazed by all I see and hear. . . . Imagine, my dear friend, if you can, a society formed of all the nations of the world: English, French, Germans . . . people having different languages, beliefs, opinions: in a word, a society without roots, without memories, without prejudices, without routines, without common ideas, without a national character. . . . What serves as a link among such diverse elements? What makes all of this into one people?" The answer to that question for the next century and a half was a uniting into a common culture based on agreed values spoken and written in a national language. That uniting was nearly shattered by a Civil War. A cause of that fearful conflict has returned in a different form to subvert that uniting.

"When you put all the hot buttons out in front of you," said political consultant Harrison Hickman in 1991, "clearly race is the one that's white hot." With decades of historical perspective behind him, the retiring executive editor of the *Washington Post*, Ben Bradlee, agreed: "The nation's most important issue is race. . . . Race remains the biggest problem." For cultural conservatives, the solution to race was not a rigid conformity to a homogeneous culture. All of us yearn, as Frankie did in *The Member of the Wedding*, to find the "*we* of me." But the "we" should not be constructed on a group solidarity of race and ethnicity but on each individual encouraged to select from options. Diversity should be defined by the diversity of individual choice, not the diversity of separate groups to which individuals are automatically assigned. Assimilation expands individual choice; counterassimilationism, the particularistic doctrine of the more zealous racial/ethnic cheerleaders, surrenders the individual to the group.

Diversity is best served through the individual connected by associations to the community rather than through the group itself creating a separate community. A tension between individual self-interest and community responsibility is natural and healthy. Racial/ethnic groups in conflict with the larger community is incendiary. Group differentiation is inevitable as we join churches and clubs, live in neighborhoods, attend college, choose a sport, and so forth. Group differentiation is destructive when it is imposed on the individual.

America has been a splendor of ideas about freedom in contending counterpoint with equality—freedom to express, freedom to possess, freedom to volunteer time and money to help others. Equality means equality before the law and an equal opportunity to better oneself. It's not a credo professed, nor acted upon, by *most* of the world's peoples.

Newcomers to the United States, seeking citizenship, partake of a fellowship of shared ideas. Longtimers by birth have always known that rituals of rededication are necessary to preserve those ideas. When things go sour, when the behavior betrays the nobility of the vision, even so, the rest of the world still wants to come over and join in. The children of those who come, born in the new land, have always been taught in the past that self-esteem is nourished, not by race and ethnicity, but by communion with a common culture. To denounce that credo of shared values, according to cultural conservatives, was a perilous threat to the meaning of America.

Race As a Visual Identifier

Race and ethnicity can scratch at the personal sensitivities of students and faculty. The old fights in the classroom about greedy businessmen and downtrodden factory workers were less personal. It is not always easy today for professors of good will to reveal evidence without offense.

Race at one time was itself a taboo subject contributing to the confusion about what it is. As an operational instrument with real-life consequences, regardless of its scientific validity, race is a visual identifier based on the physical characteristics of skin color, facial form, and eye shape. The operative test is to visit the campus cafeteria of a major university where students group themselves, not as one would expect by social class or common interests, but mostly by recognizable physical characteristics. The Caucasians are the ones with whiter skin, round eyes, thinner lips, more pointed noses, and straighter hair. The Negroes have darker skin, round eyes, flatter noses with wider nostrils, thicker lips, and woolly hair. The Orientals are yellow skinned with slanted eyes, smaller noses, and straighter hair. The Native-Americans, because of their fewer numbers on college campus, are less likely to isolate themselves on the basis of physical appearance.

The shorthand identifier for Caucasians and Negroes, or preferably African-Americans, is skin color—white and black. For Orientals, or preferably Asians, it's eye shape. There are nicknames for those who sit too frequently with the whites. Betraying blacks are Oreos—chocolate on the outside but white on the inside. Betraying Asians are Bananas—yellow on the outside but white on the inside. An apostate Native-American is an Apple—red on the outside.

What complicates the segregating propensity is that color is not a very precise identifier. People of color, assuming white is not a color, can be from the subcontinent of India, but they are not considered blacks. More immediate for the United States is where to place Hispanics. Hispanics are Caucasians but qualify for preferential treatment as a minority. So the connection between *race* and minority status is expanded to connect *ethnicity* and minority status. Which opens the bank vault of preferential treatment to any ethnic group that can lay claim to past discrimination. Which is exactly what happened at the City University of New York.

The Italian-Americans complained in 1976 that "despite the fact that Italian-Americans constitute 25% of the population of New York City, and despite a progressively increasing number of Italian-Americans graduating with a doctoral degree, the representation of Italian-Americans at the City University of New York was at a low 5% level." They persuaded the Chancellor to expand the "protected classes" under affirmative action to include Italian-Americans. Some ten years later Italian-Americans were still classified as affirmative action, but their representatives were not happy: "In 1986 only American Indians and Alaskan Natives were hired at a lower rate than were Italian-Americans." The City University of New York's discrimination policies resulted in "a de facto quota on Italian-Americans. . . ."

Quotas with timetables, or more loosely goals, are selective instruments of inclusion or exclusion. The confusion for academic administrators of good will is: Who should be classified as what? Can the appointment of a Spaniard increase the percentage of Hispanics on the faculty? Williams College tried it and protesting minority students barricaded themselves in the dean's office. Their argument: "What the college considers 'Hispanic' is really white Europeans who don't have a clue what it's like to be a Chicano or Puerto Rican." Does the college get credit towards black representation by hiring West Indians and Caribbeans? Foreign-born minorities don't count, according to Reginald Wilson of the American Council on Education. An African educated in England, Wilson maintains, may not understand the experiences of black Americans.

Language swells the confusion on campus. Whites are designated European-Americans, but that classification includes Hispanics whose national origin was the Spain of Europe. A solution is for whites to be known as Anglos with Hispanics designated non-Anglo whites. Equally muddy is the designation of Native American. In a lexical mode, William Safire explained that Native American "causes semantic difficulty because all citizens born here are native Americans, as against naturalized Americans. . . . You can't call an American Indian an Indian-American, because that refers to an immigrant from India; the accurate term for the descendant of tribespeople here before the Europeans arrived is aboriginal American, unhyphenated, meaning 'here first,' but neither that nor its hyphenated shortening, Abo-American, is catching on."

"A Backlash Against the WASP Culture. . . ."

In business, salesmen chuckle over jokes with customers to jolly them into a buying mood. In the academy, professors are not much given to telling thigh-slappers, but they have been known from time to time to pause from their labors to footnote a mood with a witticism. Making the rounds among the trusted were wordplays on gender. It doesn't get much better than "Have you heard the new Dean is renaming the department Herstory!" To which the repartee is "No, it's now His'n'Herstory." Exasperated lexicographer to an oversensitive complainer: "You can take 'man' out of 'woman' with 'womyn,' but you'll never take the 'son' out of 'person.'" Registrar to female Professor: "Go ahead, call it an ovular, but I'm classifying it a seminar!" And on the subject of sensitivity—administrator to faculty: "We must be sensitive to the feelings of short people and avoid the bigotry of Heightism. From now on we shall refer to short people as the 'vertically challenged.'"

Not too long ago jokes about ethnicity were viewed as harmless teasing. Often ethnicity was connected to religion. The traditional stop-me-if-you've-heard-this-one opened with: "There was a priest, a minister, and a rabbi. . . ." No more. "Jokes that use stereotypes are no longer funny," the *Washington Post* reported in 1991, "of course, unless they begin with 'There were these two white guys, . . .'" WASPS continue to take a heavier pounding than the band's bass drum at halftime. It's a risk, but cross cultural comparisons may be ventured if the target of jest is not an oppressed underdog:

> After completing the Grand Tour, several clergymen were relaxing in a European cafe. Over walnuts and brandy the conversation turned to the definitions of Heaven and Hell—
> *Heaven* is where the police are British, the chefs French, the mechanics German, the lovers Italian, and the organizers Swiss.
> *Hell* is where the police are German, the chefs British, the mechanics French, the lovers Swiss, and the organizers Italians.

Jocular stereotyping is a form of reckless humor in the America of the 1990s. The problem, of course, is that ethnic jokes are not respectful. If they were, we could not wash away our hostility with the refreshing springs of laughter.

A consequence of multiculturalism may be the demise of the ethnic joke on campus—or its hostile revitalization—depending on the under-

71

graduate mood during the 1990s. A survey of the humor in ethnic jokes reveals that they turn almost entirely on stereotypes. Characteristics are assigned: Poles are stupid, as are southern rednecks; Italians are inefficient as are Puerto Ricans and Mexicans; Jews are clever; WASP's are uptight; Irish are drunks; and JAP's (Jewish American Princesses) are self-indulgent.

How to tell a "dumb" joke without a group to tell it about? Dirk Johnson reported from Denver, Colorado in 1991 that "everyone knows that ethnic and racial jokes have become unacceptable in this enlightened age." So, blonds have been substituted for Poles. Sociologist Bernard Beck explained: "Wherever you go, there is a genre of dumb jokes. The only missing element is who is supposed to be dumb. What we're seeing, in a way, is a backlash against the WASP culture that once made jokes about the immigrants."

The Dilemmas

Multiculturalism in the curriculum, and its related policies in admissions and campus life, admits to no artless good-guys-bad-guys dichotomy. Solutions have a way of twisting themselves into uneasy dilemmas. The dilemmas are on-the-one-hand, on-the-other-hand choices between undesirable alternatives. On university campuses at least 11 dilemmas are tormenting students. For a nation at work—hiring, firing, and promoting—similar dilemmas can be equally troublesome.

Dilemma of Stereotyping

On the one hand, if stereotyping is used—that is, a standardized image is attached to an ethnic group—the representation is criticized as bigotry and condemned as racism.

On the other hand, if stereotyping is not used, how is it possible to make meaningful distinctions about groups in classroom discussions, to identify the differences that make a difference without which there can be no understanding? Also, is there not some truth in every stereotype, as the clergymen divined on their Grand Tour—the French *do* approach the delights of food with a reverence quite unlike the British and experienced women have testified that exuberant Italians seem to make better lovers than uptight Brits. How can teachers identify authenticity in stereotypes without being accused of intolerance?

Dilemma of Sensitivity Protection

On the one hand, if university administrators feel deeply responsible for protecting blacks, gays, and women from abusive language, they can enforce speech codes and harassment regulations against boorish offenders of campus civility. However, when is a comment perceptive observation, and when is it hurtful bigotry? How can an offender always be aware of what words are offensive to the wounded? Anyway, isn't an attempt by the administration to check opinions (as opposed to physical behavior) a perilous violation of First Amendment rights of free speech?

On the other hand, if students and teachers may speak whatever words they wish about blacks, gays, and women, isn't the spirit of the campus violated by those students and teachers, albeit scarce in number, who insist on irrational attacks on the feelings of injured groups?

Dilemma of Cultural Pluralism

On the one hand, if exalting ethnic diversity and racial solidarity is a good thing, then isn't the drift to ethnocentricism inevitable, that is, dissimilar groups are likely to be seen as inferior or at least undesirably different? Is not this promotion of group cohesion a denial of tolerance? Isn't it patronizing to identify American inventors as black or Hispanic unless every American inventor be specified by race or ethnicity? Further, should not university administrators encourage, not the racial separation of students into self-segregating social centers, but rather the clustering of students by intellectual interests, artistic activities, and intramural sports? Indeed, how is it possible to justify black colleges while condemning white colleges as racist?

On the other hand, if self-esteem is dependent on ethnic identification or racial unity, then how can the self be bolstered without supporting an ideology that emphasizes the superior nature of one's own group? How necessary is the warming oven of racial pride to bake in self-esteem?

Dilemma of Social Integration

On the one hand, if blacks and Hispanics pressure the administration to permit them to live in dormitories exclusively with other blacks or Hispanics, isn't the result a kind of segregation that neutralizes the advantages of campus diversity and pluralism? Worse, isn't the compliance with such social segregation a betrayal of the integrationist spirit of the civil rights movement?

On the other hand, if the administration refuses to permit ethnic and racial groups to retreat into protected enclaves, is it not denying Hispanics, blacks, Asians, and native Americans the comfort of kindred souls and the guidance from older friends that will ease their encounters in a world often so alien to their upbringing?

73

Dilemma of Physical Determinism

On the one hand, if color or eye shape is an approved criterion for selection in education, jobs, or marriage, then group pride is emphasized.

On the other hand, if race is a selective criterion, then the ascribed features of color and eye shape determine the destiny of an individual. Isn't that principle a violation of the democratic preference for achieved criteria, that is, what kind of human being you can become regardless of physical determinants? Further, isn't it personally offensive to be treated differently whether it be heightism measured in inches from head to toe or racism triggered by skin color and eye shape?

Dilemma of Personal Responsibility

On the one hand, if inner-city black youngsters are neglected by parents, especially fathers, and ravaged by street-life values, how can they be expected to do well in school, much less aspire to college? Indeed, rap on the street corner often condemns educational achievement as selling out to white culture. Yet, if an environmental interpretation of human behavior prevails, how can young adults be held responsible for their behavior?

On the other hand, if students are reared in wretched ghettos, can colleges, in all fairness, hold such culturally disadvantaged students to the same standards of campus behavior and classroom assignments as their more privileged classmates? To justify such special treatment, colleges must invoke a patronizing environmental determinism for human behavior.

Dilemma of Affirmative Action

On the one hand, if the playing field is not level for certified minorities, then the affirmative action of preferential admissions is necessary to give them a fair start. Especially blacks. Blacks imported as slaves, unlike other immigrant groups, were *involuntary* immigrants. Yet, affirmative action giving the advantage to blacks on the basis of race is an act of reverse discrimination against whites. A freshman class of limited enrollment is zero-sum. To let someone in is to keep someone out. Thus does the public good for one special interest group become the public bad for another, inclining whites to slink into resentment—and also to flounder in a wondering puzzlement of why a naturalized immigrant from Bolivia should get preferential treatment over a naturalized immigrant from Sweden. Is racial discrimination the way to fight racial discrimination?

On the other hand, without compensatory action to rectify past discrimination, how can blacks especially be guaranteed an equal start in life's race for achievement? And remember, colleges for generations have given preference to the children of alumni. If legacies with lower grade point averages and standardized test scores, especially the children of generous alums, get in by a non-academic criterion, and athletes by physical prowess, why not minorities on the basis of race? Why should suspecting that you were admitted as a black student seem to be more of a threat to self-esteem than getting there as a legacy or a jock? The "best black" to fill an affirmative action goal may not be the best person, but neither is a legacy necessarily the most qualified applicant. Still, isn't there an important difference between using race as a selective criterion and the family connection of a legacy or the physical skill of a jock or the brain power of a low-income applicant? Skin color or eye shape indicate the need for a *remedy* and are therefore not exalted but debasing criteria. Don't race-based remedies ironically not cure the ills of race but rather create a new illness by attaching inferior status to the indelible racial markings of skin color and eye shape?

Dilemma of Racial Features

On the one hand, if color or eye shape, for example in casting for theatrical parts, is a criterion for selection, then whites through makeup will not be able to assume the features of blacks or Asians. In colorfast casting, blacks are limited to playing Othello and whites Hamlet. But, then, won't audiences be conditioned to a color-awareness that has nothing to do with the quality of the performance?

On the other hand, if casting is color-blind, then the selection of blacks and Asians for Caucasian roles is more likely. Whites may play the Moor and blacks the Dane and audiences will soon become accustomed to color-neutrality. Still, if a color-blind policy increases the parts for minorities, doesn't it also reduce the job security of certain roles always being assigned to minorities?

Dilemma of Value Inconsistency

On the one hand, if American values teach that color should not be a selective criterion, that decent citizens should be color-blind in their attitude toward blacks and color-neutral in evaluation of individuals, then how is it possible for whites not to be bewildered when color *is* used as an evaluative criterion in legally sanctioned and morally approved cases of preferential treatment?

On the other hand, if color is not used as a criterion, how can blacks be awarded preferential rights as compensatory action for past and existing unjust treatment?

Dilemma of Dual Loyalty

On the one hand, if parents want to move beyond nostalgia for the home country and preserve in their children racial/ethnic characteristics, they will support the multiculturalists who see the curriculum as a device for reproducing in their children linguistic and cultural memories of the "mother country" and instilling a feeling of loyalty for its interests. If parents with strong ties to national origins fail to side with the multiculturalists, won't they be depriving their children of an identification that is important for their family values?

On the other hand, if affection for the country of origins is encouraged, isn't it forcing students to become hyphenated Americans, enormously complicating the exercise of American foreign policy, compelling them to endure the torment of a dual loyalty when the national interest of their country of origin does not correspond to the national interest of the United States?

Dilemma of National Unity

On the one hand, if multiculturalism, such as Afrocentricity, is rejected as a part of the educational canon, if the diversity of ethnic and racial groups is accepted but resources are not allocated for their preservation and exaltation, then isn't the faculty discrediting the richer texture of an American society which in its cultural pluralism is inexorably moving toward a more lustrous mosaic of color?

On the other hand, if the diversity in American society is accentuated, if the differences in groups are stressed, whether they be race, ethnicity, religion, class, or region, won't the *pluribus* in *e pluribus unum* overwhelm the *unum*? Could differences assume a moral dimension so powerful, as the issue of slavery in the Civil War, that the shared values that have been the glue holding together the Republic will become unstuck and diversity descend into disruptive disunion? If the danger around the globe is now more a conflict *within* nations than *between* them, from Soviet Russia and Yugoslavia in Eastern Europe to Quebec in Canada, is the Balkanizing of the United States something to worry about? Is the traditional assimilation of diverse immigrants to an essentially British heritage of Protestant values, modified by the American experience, no longer to be the approved objective? If so, with what consequences?

* * *

Every society knows its own tragedies. The American tragedy has always been first the reality and then the memory of slavery. In the dominance of Puritan-Protestantism, a tragedy presumes the existence of sin. The American tragedy was not the result of some uncontrolled fate but the collective flaw of betraying an ideal. The brute reality of slavery betrayed the shining ideal of human equality.

After the 1960s political inequality for blacks (the right to vote) became full equality. Economic (jobs) and social (housing) inequality improved markedly but continued to fall short of full equality with whites. The tragedy endures of a white majority of good will yearning to be cleansed of its sin.

The tragedy is revealed in the stories we tell each other as a people in the classroom, on campus, and in communities across the nation. One of those stories is the racial/ethnic particularisms of multiculturalism. It's a story that admits to the defeat of integration, locates its strength in separatism, sees the future in segregation. Multiculturalism's triumph is the end of assimilation. It's a story that began with the conscience to still the sound of slavery's lash and may conclude in the resentment of a white backlash.

Now can we see a show of hands?

7. STUDENTS

Students are consumers. As customers they purchase a television set from a merchant; as students they buy credits from a college. More precisely, they purchase what the credits from the college symbolize. When they have accumulated the required credits, the baccalaureate bell rings and the negotiable asset is awarded in a jubilant ceremony. And there is product differential. All institutions sell credits, but the credits vary in symbolic value depending upon the prestige of the college. A degree from a pastoral, private, selective university is worth more socially at a dinner party, and more economically in the marketplace, than the same degree and the same number of credits from a city, public, open admissions university.

Students, at the same time, are a special kind of consumer, quite unlike any other. Suggesting the numerous reasons why they are different grants us a fresh angle of vision. First, students bring to the purchasing transaction of credits required personal qualifications. Anyone can buy a television set. More than money is required to be accepted in the freshman class. The personal qualifications the student must bring to selective institutions range from academic competence and athletic ability through family wealth and ethnic diversity to residence location and personal charm.

Until liftoff in April, or thereabouts, when the post office delivers the thin envelopes (rejection) and the thick ones (acceptance), in the application ordeal all kinds of things can go wrong. Sounding El Dullo is one of them—but so is being the life of the party. The admissions staff chuckled the first time an applicant's picture smiled at them as Student of the Year from the cover of *Time*. An orthodontist's letter of recommendation to Harvard describing the brightness of his patient's restructured smile probably didn't advance the cause. An applicant to Stanford sent along a cassette in which he sang to the tune of "Don't Worry, Be Happy" "Don't Reject Me, Please Accept Me." Zzzzz.

Directors of Admissions from various places recall exchanges that prompted eyes to roll heavenward:

Furman University—"A young man completed the 'Sex' blank on our application by saying: 'Once, in Charlotte, North Carolina.'"

Lafayette College—"And why do you think that Lafayette might be a good college for you?

Candidate: Well, I don't want to go to a real big college or a real small college. I just want a mediocre college like Lafayette."

St. Lawrence University—"I remember the guidance counselor's report which arrived saying: 'Prepared in copulation with the principal.'"

Tulane University—"A conversation with a high Math, low Verbal applicant for Engineering:

Counselor: Are you a good student?

Applicant: I don't do too good in English.

Counselor: I don't do too *well* in English.

Applicant: Me neither."

Second, students are not true consumers because more than money is required to graduate with a baccalaureate. The degree has to be earned. Third, what students purchase is not a fair exchange. The services they receive are subsidized by endowments, alumni giving, and public funds.

Fourth, students as consumers are not treated equally. It costs considerably more to educate a Chemistry student than an English major. Both, however, generally pay the same tuition for a baccalaureate. Fifth, the exchange is also not "fair" because the faculty seller of credits is more powerful than the student buyer. The teacher is both the examiner of the student's classroom performance and can be the terminator of the student's academic destiny. Rigorous colleges are "should" magistrates, not "want" suppliers. Students have duties, not needs. At the same time students are not defenseless. They can independently circulate savage evaluations of teachers' personalities, publicize accusations of racist remarks, and claim sexual harassment.

Sixth, education is a profession in which the consumer does the work. Seventh, the student is both the consumer of the college's product (the curriculum) and services (sports, extra-curricular activities, social class stamping, nuptial choice augmenting, and so forth) and the output of that product and those services. Eighth, a college is paid up front before the credits are delivered. Ninth, a reputable business will stand by its product but colleges will not. General Motors will recall an automobile and replace a defective part; colleges do not recall defective alumni for reconditioning. Finally, it's *caveat emptor*. Students pay for the credits, like a television set, but there is no guarantee they get what they paid for. Anyway, colleges do not offer a warranty. Students have sued. The chances are slim that returning the credits will get your tuition back—a tradition for which the preparers of some admission office brochures can only be grateful.

A Student Consumer Movement?

If students are consumers, why no consumer movement? In business, consumers of mass products may be invited to call 800 numbers free of charge to ask questions and register complaints about a product. Indeed, in a variety of ways manufacturers seem eager to hear from their purchasers. It's part of the business ethic that it's good business to be a good guy (except in investment banking.) Manufacturers did not become good guys because they have such big hearts. The consumer movement, assisted by the regulatory powers of the government and publicized by the media, helped them to adopt such virtuous conduct.

There have been lots of movements on campus, especially since the 1960s, but they are not *consumer* movements. Civil rights, women's rights, gay rights, lifestyle rights are *ideological* protests. A consumer protest is pragmatic in its justification and specific to a product paid for.

A vigorous consumer movement has not emerged on campus in the past for several reasons. First, it's risky. You will recall that professors are not only examiners but can be terminators. Students may love their teachers, but they also fear them—as we fear anyone who has power over us. Publicly complaining about the services of professors is acting dumb, especially since there are not many professors who will join this particular crusade, unless they want to take their lunch with students in the cafeteria. Second, there's no basis for comparison. Once matriculated, students are captive to a sole-source monopoly. They don't shop around other campus classrooms and laboratories comparing who is getting a better deal. Third, reforms probably won't do the student any good. By the time a committee is named, assembled, meets, interviews, and reports, the protesting student will have graduated.

Fourth, a student consumer movement lacks a moral dimension. Right and wrong is what morality is all about. It is difficult to impose a moral dimension on allocating resources among competing constituencies when each one professes a high purpose. Is the teaching of an undergraduate a higher cause than teaching a graduate student? Is money allocated to student services and the registrar's office more moral than money assigned to a research laboratory used entirely by researchers?

Fifth, student leaders (some would call them agitators) find it difficult to focus undergraduate energies on the goal. There's nuclear power, the environment, central American politics, and grape pickers skirmishing for attention, not to mention the rights of blacks, Hispanics, Asians, women, and homosexuals. Apartheid in South Africa is a moral, international, and glamorous cause; more sections in an overenrolled course is, well, it's kind of self-seeking. POWER TO THE STUDENT CONSUMER! That's not exactly a cause you can lay down your life for.

Further, campus leaders must unite left-leaning and right-leaning forces. Student ideological protests are often an attack on, or a defense of, authority. The words are rational about authority figures, but the feelings are emotional. The justifications for attacking and defending the establishment are intellectual, but the motivations are psychological. A left-leaning sophomore deprived of the words "struggle" and "oppressed" is rendered speechless. A right-leaning junior in a solemn three-button suit at the University of AllPeople, observing five students at a sit-in being dragged from the Dean's office, is compelled to ask later about procedures. By what acceptable process, he wants to know, does the Dean intend to relent and meet the banner's demand—FREE THE UNIVERSITY OF ALLPEOPLE FIVE?

Sixth, a student consumer movement may toughen academic standards and boost class work, reducing time for fun things like parties, sports, and extracurricular activities, not to mention making it harder to graduate. A senior, looking back on his years at the University of Illinois, commented on large lectures with multiple-choice exams and minimal contact with professors: "I'm concerned that this is not just something forced on students, it's something students want because it is the easy way out. . . . we have reached the point where a student can, with a little effort, almost graduate without saying a word in class or writing a single paper." A knowledgeable friend of a private university with a superior academic reputation echoed the student's observation while reaching out to include the faculty. When asked what he thought Stanford University's most serious problems might be, he replied: "Just one. I would wonder whether this excellent, research-oriented faculty and this splendid student body with its diverse interests haven't drifted toward a kind of unwritten agreement: you don't bother us too much, we won't bother you too much."

Finally, the market value of the undergraduate degree is increased by the research distinction of the faculty. The total number of hours that the SuperStars spend with undergraduates may be miniscule. What matters is to type proudly on a resume the name of a university that stands for intellectual substance. Who will know that teaching assistants provided the intellectual substance? It may seem as sensible as learning how to swim by swimming in the same pool that championship swimmers swim in. On the other hand, it could be argued that water is not the same as atmosphere. Just sensing that in the library across campus there swells a scholar's *magnum opus* to acclaimed completion could conceivably be an inspiration for some freshmen.

Remember Bologna!

Is there enough dissatisfaction for a student consumer movement? The respected *Chronicle of Higher Education* assigned a reporter to assess the discontent. She interviewed students at more than a dozen of the country's largest research universities and concluded in early 1991 that "complaints about undergraduate education are widespread." Among her findings:

- A business major at Ohio State University stopped going to his marketing course. With more than 1,000 students in the class, he said, "all the professor could teach you was common sense." He did the readings on his own and passed the course.
- A junior at the University of Texas planned to enroll at the local community college to fulfill the requirements in the core science, language, and mathematics courses. At the university the basic courses were so crowded that professors found it difficult to spend extra time with students. She concluded that "it is too crazy to take science here when a professor doesn't have time to talk to you about genetics because he's got a class of 500."
- An armed forces veteran, enrolled at the University of Maryland at College Park, had been a translator in Korea. The teaching assistant in his first-year calculus course was Korean. "I could go up and talk to the T.A. in Korean," he reported, "but the

language problems really inhibited the other students in the class from asking questions."

- A senior in economics at the University of Minnesota's Twin Cities campus said she had never been taught by a professor during her four years at the university. While acknowledging that her case may be extreme, she added that "I am graduating from one of the best economics departments in the country and I've never had a professor." Her teachers were graduate students and part-time instructors.
- A sophomore at the University of Texas panicked when she discovered that she had to ask a faculty member to write a recommendation for her scholarship application. She found teachers to write the necessary references but "they hardly know me."

In the list of student complaints none sounds more sorrowful than the exposure to teaching assistants. After three years of self-examination, the University of California at Berkeley concluded that "the key difference between those students who were very satisfied with their experience at Berkeley and those who were not was the quality of their contacts with faculty and graduate teaching assistants."

Teaching assistants are mostly untrained, unsupervised, and under stress to finish their doctorate. At least three states have passed legislation that college and university teachers must be proficient in English—a policing function by a state official that must be humiliating for the trustees of targeted institutions in those states of Pennsylvania, Florida, and Michigan. Still, with foreigners representing 46% of the full-time graduate students in engineering and 26% in science, it's not surprising that understanding the teacher is a problem. A bigger problem for the future of a competitive United States is what the statistic reveals about scientific training and its relation to the entire American educational system.

Does the litany of lamentations about class size, overenrolled required courses, incompetent academic advising, unavailable professors, disinterested part-time instructors, and unintelligible teaching assistants suggest the beginnings of a student consumer movement? "We're seeing students be more vocal on their insistence on high quality in all aspects of their educational experience," reported the dean of students at the University of Toledo. "They're acting in a way like consumers. They're saying: "I'm paying top dollar for an education and I expect to get it."

Protests in public universities against tuition hikes and budget cuts are not new. Public universities, spearheaded by the students, have frequently competed for funding with welfare mothers, automobile-punishing potholes, children's books for the local library, and art teachers for the public school system. What is a "just" share of available tax monies? *The new direction in the student consumer movement is not fighting for a share of legislative funding but inquiring about how that share is allocated and used effectively on campus.* At Syracuse University Professor William D. Coplin, who teaches public policy, helped students found Undergraduates for a Better Education (UBE) and then used the pressure group to teach them the complexities of shaping public policy.

UBE's more sophisticated consumer movement was not above showmanship. It conducted a survey identifying factors limiting the quality of undergraduate education at Syracuse. The results were publicized in a flyer posted all over the campus during Parents' Weekend. The flyer's headline: ARE YOU GETTING WHAT YOU PAY FOR? The administration rolled with the punch and began to work with the students.

Coplin, as both faculty adviser to UBE and curriculum designer of a public policy course, makes two points valuable for not only students but parents, alumni, trustees, and legislators. One is the necessity to understand the structure, or what we have been defining as the culture, of the university. "Students who have joined UBE tend to first think that the problem is merely caused by some incompetent administrators and faculty who are insensitive to their needs. They leave realizing that the problem is structural—that is, it permeates the attitudes and therefore the institutions of the entire University community including students, parents, alumni, politicians, and the public along with faculty and administrators. They learned how attitudes like 'publish or perish' on the part of the faculty and administration combined with the pervasive grade-grubbing attitudes of most students diminished the quality of their education. They also learned that their fellow students were as much a part of the problem and solution as the faculty and administrators."

Coplin's other valuable point centers on process. "The most important lesson that the members of UBE appeared to have learned is that the essence of the democratic process is to stop whining and start acting. At first, they were hesitant about their right to express themselves. Several kept saying, 'What will my parents say when I get kicked out of school?' Eventually they realized that Deng Xiaoping was not running the University and that if nothing else, freedom of expression is respected. . . . They also realized that the rulers—in this case the faculty and administrators—could be influenced by a combination of solid arguments and careful political strategies."

The nascent student consumer movement is not defined by lawless acts blocking entrances to classrooms or by multiple demands embarrassing to the university administration. There have been, however, imaginative flourishes that barely remain within the boundaries of civility. When Michael Levine, former head of New York Air, became the dean of Yale's School of Organization & Management, he abruptly redirected the approach of the professional program. Outraged alums hired an airplane to fly over the graduation ceremony towing a banner. The banner's ominous message: BOESKY. MILKEN. LORENZO. LEVINE. ALL RAIDERS WILL FALL. Levine has survived.

The essence of consumer discontent is the feeling of being shortchanged. After enduring an unsatisfactory course thrice weekly for over three months, students have struck back with an instrument that the university is supposed to be teaching them to use with effect—the power of the pen. In rogue publications evaluating faculty performance, a maladroit professor stands before the glistening blade of wit like a fattened turkey in November.

Pedagogical critiques follow and may be invoked by readers for deserving purposes:

- The best thing about Professor Mumbles course is when it was over.
- For those of you who missed Professor Mumbles course last year, this is your golden opportunity. You can miss it again.
- If you asked me what the course was about, I would say it was about as much as I could take.
- Professor Mumbles can breathe easily this semester. With the appearance of Professor Dullard, his course is no longer the worst taught at the university.
- The best thing about Professor Mumbles' lectures was when he said: "And finally."
- When a student taking Professor Mumbles' course was asked whether he had heard his last lecture, he sighed: "I hope so."
- Some people can stay longer in an hour than others in a week—which is how most students felt about time spent in his class.

- When it was reported that Professor Mumbles had died, one of his students asked: "How can you tell?"
- One student grumbled that halfway through Professor Mumbles lecture he felt like the frustrated baseball manager who shouted at an umpire: "Are you gonna get any better, or is *this* it?"

If the student consumer movement needs a rallying cry, how about REMEMBER BOLOGNA! In the Middle Ages, at Bologna University in northern Italy, students engaged professors in something like a contractual relationship. If the professor fulfilled the specifications agreed upon, he got paid. Otherwise, *he* paid. At Bologna, if a professor wished to be absent from class for a day, he had to request and receive permission from the students. Should he wish to leave town, he was required to deposit a sum of money as security for his return. "By the city-regulations, moreover, for each day on which he failed to secure an audience of five for an ordinary lecture . . . he was treated as absent and incurred the appointed fine accordingly." There's more.

"In medieval as in modern times lecturers had a tendency to spend a disproportionate time over the earlier portions of a book, and so leave none for the rest," explained Hastings Rashdall in *The Universities of Europe in the Middle Ages.* "With a view to checking this practice, an expedient was adopted at Bologna . . . . The law-texts were divided into portions known as *puncta;* and the doctor was required to have reached each *punctum* by a specified date. At the beginning of the academical [sic] year he was bound to deposit the sum of 10 Bologna pounds with a banker, who promised to deliver it up at the demand of the rectors. For every day that the doctor was behind time, a certain sum was deducted from his deposit. . . ."

REMEMBER BOLOGNA!

8. TUITION—STICKER PRICE

Tuition at selective universities and colleges has been rising faster than inflation primarily because the demand for a prestigious degree is greater than the supply. It takes not years but decades, really half centuries, to create a university that can boast a nationally prestigious degree. For an international reputation it takes a century. A college is like a museum. Like the paintings on the walls, it takes a long time to put together a collection of faculty and buildings, style and reputation.

At prestigious universities the demand has increased markedly over the supply. The admissions statistics at Princeton University, even with its traditional focus on individual instruction and small class size, are not unusual. The Dean of Admissions calculates that 25 years ago 33% of the applicants for Princeton's Class of 1964 were admitted. For the class of 1992, 17% of the applicants were admitted. The cut to half is the more striking when the increased size of the classes are factored in—from 833 to 1,130.

Establishing a reputation for short supply and high demand is crucial for an attractive market value. The market value of the degree is crucial. "What it's worth depends on the college," explained Amanda Williams, a junior at New Jersey's Montclair State College. "I'd be willing to pay more for a better reputation. What do I mean? Well, if I went to Harvard and I was competing for a job with someone from Montclair State, who do you think would get it?" Harvard may cost more, but it is a sound investment. The child worthy of such an investment now includes sister as well as brother. In an increasingly gender-free society, it is believed she deserves an equal chance. However worthy a value, it is an expensive one for mom and dad to honor—which many do by a two-paycheck family.

Tuition does not respond sensitively to market forces because selective universities enjoy an oligopoly on prestige. They engage each year in cost-plus pricing. The usual procedure is to determine what the qualified buyers will pay from their combined assets, income, and loans and then budget the costs. The top private universities start with requests from the campus, work up the budget, and then set the asking price for the credits.

Universities share with certain kinds of businesses the practice of price discrimination. That is, an identical service is offered to different buyers at different prices even though the service costs the same. Businesses give a better price when the purchasing volume is high, or the buyer's credit is good. Universities give a better price for their credits when the buyer offers unequal personal attributes—he or she is bright, athletic, poor, or minority ethnic. Paying the full price are the dumb, rich, wimpish, or child of an alumnus or alumna.

Thus are the rich soaked to pay for the education of the poor. It's all part of the American creed of people being created equal—not equal in ability but equal before the law and as much as possible with equal opportunity. It is sometimes perplexing for Europeans with a different class system and set of values to understand why wealthy Americans endow student scholarships so the less privileged can compete with their own children for places in selective universities and for seats among the mighty. But Americans, especially self-made men, create student scholarships with immense pride, though they may not always recognize that the greater the institutional endowment, the higher the tuition they will have to pay for their own children—if admitted.

By any sensible economic principle, lots of money in the university's stock and bond portfolio *should reduce tuition.* One reason why the reverse is true is that the endowment is used to admit highly qualified students who can't afford the tuition—as well as buying, of course, distinguished research professors. So, the greater the endowment, the better the students and professors and the higher the tuition in a market willing to support an ascending spiral.

Indeed, higher education since World War II is a testament to the American egalitarian value of equal access earned by merit. For example, in the Ivy League during the depression 1930s, if the body was warm and the check was good, you were in—especially if you were what is now known as a "Preppie." In the decades after the war, the Ivies continued to admit qualified boys, and then girls, from private (or as they preferred to be called, "independent") preparatory schools. To a far greater extent, however, they matriculated multitudes of applicants from public schools.

The Ivies in the decades after the war instituted to a greater degree than in the past what might be called progressive tuition. In a progressive income tax, the rich hand over to the government a greater percentage of their income than the poor—or at least are supposed to. Well, progressive tuition is the same. Tuition is set high as a way of making the rich pay more while student aid reduces the net tuition of the poor.

Softening the Sticker Shock

Private universities and colleges, not unlike your local car dealer, post a sticker price. Sticker shock is softened by a discounting variable. For highly selective institutions, like those in the Ivy League, the discounting variable is scholarships based entirely on economic need. Applicants are so numerous that it is unnecessary for campuses to use scholarship money to buy quality students. Parents must endure a financial striptease as colleges put their assets through a pitiless wringer of analysis. Thus does parent/child willingness to make the sacrifice to pay what they are judged to be able to pay contribute to the annual academic drama of selecting, accepting, and rejecting.

Less prestigious private colleges and universities soften sticker shock with a discounting variable called a "merit scholarship." Applicants don't actually cut a deal because there is no direct negotiation, but their personal attributes are weighed by the college with corresponding scholarship assistance.

Putting together a package of tuition, loans, grants, and part-time work has forced colleges to become financial advisors. They have also become shrewd merchandisers. Colleges, emerging from a tradition that promotion is uncouth, have decided it's now couth. A few have even leveraged their assets as collateral at the local bank so their students can get loans at a reduced rate of interest. It's a supplement that sweetens the package.

In business price fixing, even price leadership, can be a punishable no-no. In higher education, tuition hikes march upward in a chain reaction with institutions knowing their place in the pecking order. Administrators are careful not to get out of line with their competitors in the annual pricing boost. The lockstep prompted the Justice Department to begin an antitrust investigation into possible collusion among certain institutions in the setting of tuition, student aid, and faculty salaries.

In 1991 the Justice Department charged eight Ivy League universities and the Massachusetts Institute of Technology with violating the Sherman Antitrust Act by illegally conspiring to restrain price competition on financial aid to prospective students. This was the way it worked: The Ivies and MIT got together with other prestigious institutions with inelastic demand curves. Together they decided how much each family would pay towards tuition. Each student who had been accepted by more than one institution in the group was assigned a "family contribution" which in effect was the real price of attending the school.

Attorney General Dick Thornburgh rebuked the Ivies: "Students and their families are entitled to the full benefits of price competition when they choose a college. This collegiate cartel denied them the right to compare prices and discounts among schools, just as they would in shopping for any other service. The defendants conspired to eliminate cost competition as a factor in choosing a college. The choice of whether to consider price when picking a school belongs to parents and students, not the college or university."

The Ivies filed a consent decree and said they wouldn't do it anymore. They also said they wouldn't do anymore what they claimed they had not been doing which was to discuss and agree on increases in tuition and faculty salary. (MIT chose to fight.) There was a lot of hurt feelings. The Ivies claimed they were acting in consort for God, country, and students. Tuition based on agreed need, not merit, certified that limited funds went to the neediest students. The Ivies vowed to continue doing independently what they had done collectively—award financial aid strictly on the basis of need. Would the change set off a free-market bidding war for the most choice candidates? Congress could expect a lobbying effort to reinterpret antitrust statutes.

Private colleges of lesser prestige, in contrast with the Ivies, keep tuitions high and then discount the published tuition price with merit scholarships in addition to aid based on need. The stratagem increases matriculants with higher Scholastic Aptitude Test scores. As the SAT average for the college rises, so does the prestige. Additionally, if the tuition is high, like an expensive automobile, the education is presumed to be good.

As the tuition charged by a private college rises, so does its ranking defined by economic class and social class. Economic class is measured by money. Social class is revealed in your personal style—the way you dress, move about, handle yourself, the accent and the words you use. It includes your family lineage which is elevated by money if the money is mellowed by time. The economic and social class background of the student body enhances the desirability of a college. In some cultures the aspiring might find such human endowments intimidating. In American society, a nation of hustlers, if you're going to be mobile, better be upward. And if you are already in the upper middle or upper classes, it's an unhappy family that sends a child off to a college less prominent than the one the parents attended.

Robin Hood robbed the rich to give to the poor. By a delightful irony, rich alumni do not discourage their alma mater from playing Robin Hood in a Sherwood Forest crowded with applicants. After all, as we noted, the higher the tuition, then the more valuable the institution is thought to be. And the more valuable the institution, the more valuable the alumni degree must be both socially and economically.

Tuition-paying parents know it, too. The quarrels between middle class (especially upper middle class) parents and their children about college choice frequently begin with a disagreement about the importance of status. True, upper middle class parents want their child to "get a good education" but in an institution with eminence. Since that eminence is largely achieved, not by teaching their child, but by faculty scholarship, why should parents question the allocation of resources to scholarship? A reputation for academic distinction, after all, determines the value of the degree they are sweating to pay for. Anyway, parents are not taught in populous universities by inexperienced teaching assistants or required to sit through tedious lectures. Students are.

Colleges that stress teaching are sometimes deliciously rewarded with negative comments about the larger doctorate-granting universities. Harvard, of course, is simply monumental, the summit towards which universities gaze in reverence, the peak to appraise an aspiring ascent to national eminence. Cantabridgian arrogance is fed by the verity that it is a tough, competitive cockpit of academic excellence. Thus is it a measure of some comfort to colleges of a more intimate scale, boasting of their close student-faculty contacts, when the advantages of their niche are confirmed by a Harvard graduate of some authority. *The New York Times* reported in 1990 that Harvard might have to take a hard look at itself when President Bok retired the following year: "James O. Freedman, the president of Dartmouth College and also a graduate of Harvard, said the biggest challenge would be *improving teaching for undergraduates, a perpetual student complaint at Harvard*. 'It is very hard in a large research institution to place adequate emphasis on undergraduate teaching,' Mr. Freedman said. 'That's the challenge of Harvard's next decade.'" Ah, for Williams and Amherst and Haverford and Bryn Mawr and all the rest, that's following your bliss!

9. TUITION—COSTS AND BENEFITS

Business and education are sharply dissimilar in the way they evaluate performance. At a business doing well, employees, as the holiday season approaches in December, hope to get a *bonus*. (At non-profit organizations in December, you're asked for a *donation!*) A business knows it's doing a good job if it enjoys a favorable return on investment and increases its earnings per share of stock. You can put a number on it. Dollar profits are both the subjective motivation of effort and the objective measurement of performance.

Adapting tested business concepts to understand how higher education operates is perilous for a college president. It only convinces the faculty that the president is no longer of the gown, rather like a wayward man of the cloth who has taken up with moneychangers. Referring to a college as a "service industry" makes it sound like a line of work no better than any other. "Market share" seems so vulgar—as if colleges were competitively scratching for talented applicants like crass television networks targeting upscale viewers. Calling students "direct consumers" cheapens learning. Referring to society as "indirect consumers" of scholarly research may be perceptive, but it is rather inelegant. "Variable pricing" is suspicious because it sounds like some courses may not only be more expensive than others but worth more. Analyzing faculty workloads in terms of "productivity units" reduces the nobility of faculty labor to a crude counting by numbers. Entering into "growth compacts" with faculty in their teaching and research activities is an invasion of privacy. "Teacher training" is something public school teachers do. "Information systems" must be some dreadful plan imposed by an accounting mentality to crush the inquiring spirit.

Where the general faculty is not involved, specifically in housekeeping activities, strict accounting systems have been incorporated. The purchasing of supplies, payroll procedures, and maintenance operations are often sharply managed. Many colleges have wisely subcontracted food services to independent enterprises.

For the twin missions of the university—teaching and scholarship—resistance to a translation of business concepts to the academy remains. It must be recalled that most academics consciously rejected business as a career. Businessmen chase vulgar goals with rude means. Above them are academics pursuing the nobler goal of truth with intellect and sensibility. Remember what those consultants, probably faculty from the business college, did to the local symphony orchestra:

> The four oboe players have nothing to do for unacceptable periods of time. Their numbers should be reduced, and the work spread more evenly over the entire symphony. The reallocation will eliminate peaks of activity.

> Too many first violins were playing identical notes. This is unnecessary duplication. The staff should be cut. If a large volume of sound is necessary, use an electronic amplifier.

> There is too much repetition of some musical passages. Scores should be pruned. No useful purpose is served by the horns repeating a passage that has already been played by the strings.

The barbarians cut costs and wrecked the orchestra.

A Full Product Line

A *profit-and-loss analysis* assumes that a business tries to make money directly. American capitalist ideology asserts that business indirectly does good in the process. Rotarians assure us that "he profits most who serves best." Money is a measure of the service provided.

A university tries to do good directly and that makes everything very complicated. How do you measure doing good directly? Can a minister calculate in quantitative terms the virtue of saving a single soul? Can an environmentalist measure the worth of a species once endangered and now safely surviving? Can a university put a number on the future contribution of a graduating senior who has majored in philosophy?

A *cost-benefit analysis* is a useful instrument as a point of departure. However, cost-benefit analysis is muddled because colleges insist on offering a "full product line." A university specializing in engineering will include departments in botany, political science, and art history. Colleges within an easy commute of each other have tried cooperating—you offer our sociology courses and we'll do your history. But collegial decision making makes the reallocation of resources more difficult than in business. Job security is a delicate issue in a tenured occupation, especially when the tenured share so powerfully the governance of the occupation.

Budget-shrewd presidents who risk more than annual trial balloons about "focusing" resources become job-imperiled presidents. The mythology of the elite university decrees that it continue to serve as the institutional equivalent of the "Renaissance person." It is, after all, the only institution where all learning can find a protected home. To cut a department is to dismember, to tear, to slice at the organic whole of the college.

Also indispensable to a prestigious university is a full service library. Every field in each department insists on ordering the current journals, if not to read now, to be available for future study. Books are one-of-a-kind products and must be purchased from sole-source publishers. Not only is the inventory carried over every year but never ceases expanding. An old book is not "obsolete merchandise" but a piece of information valuable for future research. So, librarians welcome the computer's gift of mass data storage but must still preserve infrequently used books in low-cost warehouses. From the warehouse individual volumes are trucked to the main library in response to reader requests. Expansion is expensive, even when it's compression.

Costs and Benefits

If a cost-benefit analysis lacks the cleanliness of a profit-and-loss statement, we can at least ask some tough questions of universities. What are the benefits of a university education? If a degree at one university costs three times more than at another, is the degree three times as beneficial? Why has tuition increased faster than the inflation rate? What costs should be assigned to undergraduate education?

What are the benefits of a university education? The most important benefit, ironically, is not the one promoted. University's boast of the absolute excellence of their graduating final product. Top-drawer rank as a university is not established by the relative excellence of the student measured in the progress from freshman to senior years. Following this kind of *value-added* objective is the beginning of a slide into second-rate status. Colleges trumpet the *absolute quality* of their graduates—and their alumni. Alumni cooperate. They do not cite in their resume how their alma mater molded a sorry piece of clay into something better. It's their *absolute* performance as a student that's promoted, not their relative improvement from freshman to senior years. Personal best may celebrate a measurable achievement satisfying to the self. Comparative best pays off in a competitive world keyed to achievement.

A university education over the decades has been increasingly beneficial in economic terms. If a graduating senior may, with apologies, be referred to as an "output," then the earning power of that output can be measured against the graduated output of a high school. In 1970 full-time male workers who were college graduates earned an average of 39% more than high school graduates. By 1989 the advantage had jumped to 45%. Even after accounting for tuition, living expenses and lost earnings while in college, higher education is still a profitable investment. The decline of high school graduate earning power may account for some increase in the college graduate advantage. The gloss on the point, however, does not diminish the higher take-home pay that the baccalaureate sheepskin commands.

A university is supposed to help students do at least the following:

Think logically with words and numbers

Write and talk clearly

Respond aesthetically

Establish a moral framework

Embark on a journey of lifelong learning

If these are minimum academic objectives (there are also social and physical objectives in residential institutions), then the degree to which these objectives have been achieved indicates the quality of the university's performance. Objectives measured against academic performance make accountability possible. We do know how universities perform in preparing students for professional and graduate schools. To get into a medical or law school generally requires taking a national entrance test. About one quarter of graduating seniors enroll in graduate or professional schools. What of the other three quarters? We *do not* know what kind of a job universities are doing with them—and that may be just as well for the peace of mind of those concerned about the destiny of the Republic. In the public schools of the nation, the fight to make teaching accountable is whether what students should know and be able to do are measurable in a national test. Public schools are not the only institutions that resist making the presumed immeasurable accountable by translating it into something measurable. Why not include colleges and universities in the proposal for national testing?

The lack of measurable information makes selecting a university an exercise in feel and hunch. There are dozens of guidebooks to colleges and universities. "The guidebooks offer a wealth of information," the

National Endowment for the Humanities' Lynne Cheney has concluded, "except when it comes to the single thing most important to know when choosing a school: the quality of undergraduate education." There is, of course, the videotape of the campus. Is that the university president? No, he just looks like Lee Iacocca coming towards us punching home the message that the University of UBelongHere builds quality into each of its fortunate students?

Is it more beneficial to get an education in the state of New York at Columbia or the State University of New York at Buffalo, in Texas at Rice or the University of Texas at Austin, in California at the University of Southern California or the University of California at Los Angeles, in North Carolina at Duke or the University of North Carolina at Chapel Hill? All are distinguished research institutions voted into the prestigious Association of American Universities.

The full tuition for a state resident at the first institution listed for each state can be three times as much as the second institution. Is an undergraduate education at Columbia, Rice, the University of Southern California, or Duke three times as beneficial than at the State University of New York at Buffalo, the University of Texas at Austin, the University of California at Los Angeles, or the University of North Carolina at Chapel Hill? The quality of the faculty is about the same with similar salaries. The physical plants within each state are not markedly better. So, too, the climate (except, maybe, rain-laden Buffalo). In some places there may be more individual attention and a smaller teacher-student ratio, but not to a multiple of three. So why pay more?

Students pay three times more for an education at the first named institutions rather than attend the second because the first named are private institutions. Students come from wealthier backgrounds. The social class markings that the degree brings is an escalator to a more successful life after graduation. It is not so much the educational experience as the social class identification that is the payoff. It's what the degree connected to the name of the institution stands for. The endowment of social class is the selective private university's major asset.

Whether advantages add up to a multiple of three is like asking if an expensive sports car is worth three times as much as a Ford sedan. The utility value of speed and comfort is hardly three times as great. Indeed, economy of operation and cost of insurance would seem to make the Ford more desirable than the expensive sports car. The sports car and the Ford tell a different story about their owners. The motivation for going to a high-tuition private university or buying an expensive sports car may indeed be a search for quality, but the consequences of the purchase are an increase in status.

The university has its own cost-benefit analysis. The cost is name professors, the celebs in their field respected by their peers for scholarship. The benefits are academic distinction for the university. Undergraduates have their own cost-benefit analysis. The cost is tuition. The benefits are what the degree can command in the marketplace of an entry-level job and the pecking order of social class rank. Those benefits must be worth the tuition for those who can pay it, or they wouldn't pay it. Whether the high tuition delivers *an educational experience* three times as beneficial must await a value-added measurement of a student's progress from freshman to senior years.

If classroom experience were the only value inherent in the earning of a baccalaureate, the biggest educational bargain in America is the community college. The tuition difference between two years at a community college and two years at a private university can be ten times. Is the teaching ability of a professor at a research university ten times more effective than the teacher in a community college? Some would argue that the community college professors on the average are preferable because of their devotion to teaching. Further, 19% of full-time community college teachers now hold a doctorate. The irony is that students at private research universities are paying *ten times more* for a course taught by a teaching assistant who may be *less credentialed* than the community college professor. The community college professor not only holds regular office hours for academic advising but is also paid something like three times more per course than the graduate student teaching assistant.

There are close to 1,000 public community colleges in the United States. No two are alike in their blend of administrative leadership, faculty skill, student character, and physical plant. What they all share in common is an inexpensive price tag. At the better ones it could be argued that graduating sophomores, moving on to their junior and senior years at a four-year university, are carrying with them 60 transferable credits of unashamed quality, especially in the basic courses of mathematics, science, and languages. The price per credit is a bargain, but like life, there is more to being an undergraduate than cashing in on bargains.

"It Is Better to Have Come and Loafed . . . ."

A baccalaureate is not just 120 credits representing time spent in classrooms and laboratories. In residential colleges and universities, the life of the campus in its social, sports, and extra-curricular activities shapes the personality of the student. An admissions officer is seldom so gross as to emphasize two advantages of his or her campus—one is a championship team (preferably football or basketball), the other is the social class standing that was touched upon above. The university is not supposed to be about sports and status, but of course it is. The emphasis on sports in many large research universities has been thoroughly denounced in numerous commentaries. We here continue the search for the benefits of social class which have received less attention.

A discussion of social class is embarrassing for Americans. Social class intrigues most cultures and some, like the British, are obsessed by it. Americans like to talk about economic class. Economic class is based on money—which is not really a part of the person and can be lost as well as gained. Social class is based not so much on becoming but on being. It also carries with it ascribed characteristics that are objectionable to an egalitarian ethic—family background, sometimes referred to as "breeding," old rather than nouveau wealth, and a fashion of speaking.

John Grier Hibben, the president of Princeton University during the 1920s, was reported to have said, and if he didn't he should have, that "it is better to have come and loafed than never to have come at all." Emulating the style without the intellectual substance is better than no style at all. Universities range in function from offering a non-stop nuptial bazaar to boundless opportunities to refine the intellect. No function is more transforming than the university playing Henry Higgins to the annual arrival of freshmen Eliza Doolittles. Pygmalion, you will recall, fell in love with the fair lady he created in sculpture. Aphrodite brought her to life for him. The faith that there will be a transformation of teenagers into fair ladies and the metamorphosis of raw boys into polished gentlemen is an unspoken contribution of campus life. It's one reason why parents and students, as we suggested earlier, are willing to pay more for one university than another. Should the transformation fail to take place, there is still the class-typing reputation that the badge of the university's degree commands in the marketplace and at the country club.

10. TUITION—WHERE IT GOES

Why did tuition increase faster than the rate of inflation during the 1980s? In the 1980s average tuition rose an inflation-adjusted 67% at private universities, 46% at public universities, and 58% at other private four-year schools.

In 1986, 58% of the American people said they thought a college degree was very important in order to get a job or to advance in a career. By 1991 the number had jumped to 73%. Should we not marvel at the restraint exercised by our educational leaders over the past decade? Connect the high value attached to their product with excessive demand hammering at the short supply of places available at private prestigious institutions. Why did our educational retailers behave with such commendable moderation? Could we have counted on the average store-keeper to have been equally restrained if tempted with such de-mand-supply imbalances? Was it compassion for the rich, who could have afforded to pay double the full tuition? Or was it prudence? Might boost-ing the tuition even higher have incited investigations?

Academic accounting is pretty much like everyone's household budget. It's easy enough to specify where the money comes from; it's where it *goes* that's the problem. On the *income side,* if the budget is balanced, a loss of revenue from one source has to be offset by an increase from another source. If certain revenues decline, e.g., govern-ment aid for students or alumni contributions, there will be a shortfall. In private universities that cannot draw on state funding, increasing tuition is the fallback position to a shortfall in revenues.

To fatten income, both private and public universities are multiplying ways to rent their facilities for outside use. A persistent dream is to connect with corporations for mutual benefit. Most people have sexual fantasies; Directors of Development dream in patent fantasies which emerge from university laboratories in cooperation with market-savy corporations.

103

The *expenditure side* can be divided into two classifications—costs and enhancements. *Costs* are obvious. If a journal for the library increases its price, costs will increase. Faculty salaries increased faster than the inflation rate during the 1980s, but not because professors were making a killing. Actually, faculty were playing catch-up so that by 1990 salaries in constant dollars were about the same as in the mid-1970s. A cost is also money that must be spent to stay even with the competition. Computers were a big cost during the 1980s.

The cost to repair a leaking roof is the same whether it protects students or factory workers. There are, however, costs that are peculiar to every industry. In academia, the jargon requiring definition is an FTE. An FTE is a full-time equivalency student. An FTE generally takes 15 credits a semester. Three students, each taking five credits, will equal one FTE. Careful budgeteers will allow for an increase of costs with an increase of part-time students. An FTE consisting of three students means three records in the registrar's office, not one.

Enhancements are expenditures that upgrade the quality of the university. There are enhancements that would not require increasing tuition to meet the additional expenditures. A wealthy alumnus gives an earth sciences laboratory with, the financial officer hopes, a maintenance endowment for upkeep. A corporation endows a chair in economics with, one hopes, enough to pay for secretarial help beyond the professor's salary and fringe.

Enhancements that increase the operating budget are a conference to call attention to the university's recent arrival among the players in the earth sciences or an office to house the new chair in economics. The Chairperson of the History Department lays it on the line to the president: Either we come up with $10,000 more per year for RisingStar and cut his teaching load by a third, or he's out of here by spring and off to the University of Big Bucks where they have just discovered a massive oilfield under the men's dormitory. What takes place is something the president of a university cannot tolerate: It's no longer a question of staying even with the competition but falling behind in the prestige race. In business, it's the equivalent of losing money. Unlike a business, the bad news does not appear on next year's balance sheet. But the word gets around that the History Department at Faltering U. has lost RisingStar. There are even reports that graduate students, like wise men of old, are leaving to follow RisingStar. RisingStar was known to have harbored messianic fantasies, the student newspapers reported. Was that truly He sighted walking on the lake not far from the boathouse?

Clearly, the president, confronted with dozens of departmental chairpersons clamoring for additional funding, cannot afford to be the president of a doomed university. When the financial officer says there is no money for the conferences, the salary raises, and the adjunct teachers to replace RisingStar in the classroom, the president says sure there is: Raise tuition and let the undergraduates pay for it. And why not, since the demand of qualified applicants far exceeds the supply of places available. Indeed, in prestigious universities, increasing tuition may *increase* the number of applicants, since high tuition is an indication of superior quality.

The transaction recalls John Wesley's command translating self-seeking capitalism into beneficent Christianity—"gain all you can, save all you can, give all you can." For prestigious universities, it's "charge all you can, cry all you can, and spend all you can." The charging and the crying and the spending are all for a good cause—increasing the distinction of the university through the hiring and retaining of scholars who will contribute to knowledge in their respective fields.

During the decade of the 1980s, average tuition in constant dollars at private universities for those paying full tuition more than doubled. Where did all that money go? Which to costs and which to enhancements?

Enhancements, as indicated, are upgrades. Enhancements are increasing the library budget in constant dollars by 10%, hiring a "name" scholar for 20% more than the salary of a retiring professor, or reducing the teaching load of a sought-after SuperStar threatening to decamp for more solicitous premises.

A massive enhancement is an across-department reduction in faculty teaching loads. The reduction in teaching loads from twelve to nine or six hours per week has one *definite enhancement* and one *indefinite enhancement*. The university definitely remains competitive with other universities as a desirable place to work. The indefinite enhancement is whether the reduction of teaching hours will represent a corresponding increase in published research contributing to the university's prestige. A *definite consequence* is an increase in instructional costs. More professors, part-time adjuncts, or teaching assistants have to make up for the one-third reduction in teaching hours. Using part-timers or TA's is the cheapest way to go, but they don't contribute to the scholarly distinction of the university. *Increasing the number of full-time, tenure-track professors with a recognized reputation for scholarship in their field, or a potential for distinction, is the key to enhancement.*

What has been happening in universities is an enhancement of massive proportions. At the same time there have been heavy losses in instructional productivity. *More* professors were hired to service *fewer* students. In the years from 1977 to 1987 in higher education the number of full-time students in the arts and sciences *decreased* by 14% while the full-time faculty in the arts and sciences *increased* by 16%!

If costs are necessary expenditures to conduct the enterprise, and enhancements discretionary expenditures to elevate the reputation of the university, who shall decide what is a cost and what is an enhancement? Costs are mandated ramps for wheelchairs or specialists to run the computer center. But is a minority counselor hired to meet the needs of Asian students a cost necessary to make the institution run effectively, or is it an enhancement? Expenditures assigned to costs and those to enhancements have to be negotiated taking into consideration the special conditions of each campus.

To explain tuition increases above the inflation rate, are costs or enhancements the more powerful? The answer to that depends on who is trying to explain what to whom. To outraged parents who have just taken out a second mortgage on their house, university presidents are going to plead two explanations—there has been a shortfall in other sources of revenue and campuses must meet costs, which by their very nature exceed the inflation rate, i.e. the labor-intensive nature of teaching. The emphasis in this study on enhancements is only because the educational establishment has tended to focus on costs as an explanation for tuition hikes above the inflation rate.

Cooking the Numbers?

What costs should be assigned to undergraduate education? To soften the annual blow of a rise in tuition, universities politely affirm that undergraduates pay for only a percentage of their education. That may be true. If so, the questions to ask are: What percentage of their education do undergraduates actually pay for? What expenditures are included in that percentage figure?

An annual accounting statement describing a university's operation, like a household budget, is divided into two classifications. There are revenues (sources), and there are expenditures (uses).

On the *revenue* side stands:

Tuition (undergraduate, graduate, and professional)

Endowment income

Gifts from alumni and others

Government/foundation/corporate grants

Auxiliary enterprises, e.g., dormitory rents

Direct appropriations from state governments (in public and in some private institutions)

On the *expenditure* side stands:

Instruction and departmental research

Sponsored research, e.g., a separate laboratory not connected with undergraduate instruction

Medical School—if the university carries the heavy expenses of a medical school, it often commands its own budget line.

Student services, e.g., admissions, counselling, extra-curricular activities

Student aid, e.g., institutionally funded scholarships

Administration

Auxiliary enterprises, e.g., painting the dormitories

Operation and maintenance of plant

Academic support, e.g., the library

Student aid is usually carried as an expenditure. A more precise disclosure, however, would list scholarships as a *discount on tuition*. Knocking a thousand dollars off the tuition of a needy student is no more an expenditure than an automobile dealer discounting a thousand dollars off the sticker price.

Placing student aid in expenditures has at least one important consequence for both public and private universities. In *public* universities, students sometimes noisily protest tuition increases. What if tuition increases were tied to per-student costs? Like indexing social security payments to the cost of living, indexing tuition to per-student costs is automatic. Indexing is bliss for state governors. The automatic transaction banishes the politically perilous decision of whether each year to raise tuition to close the budget gap. If student aid is a discount on tuition, rather than an expenditure, it makes attempts at calculating the cost per student more precise.

In *private* universities, some parents may wonder if what the university says they are paying for is actually what they are paying for. Removing tuition from the expenditures side reduces the amount of money spent by the university on their child's education and therefore the cost-per-student.

What percentage of instructional costs does tuition pay for? Are universities cooking the numbers? (In business, commingling or misappropriating funds is a felony.) Estimates of tuition meeting the instructional budget range from 25% for public to 80% for private doctorate-granting universities. Many private prestigious universities remind their alumni that they paid for only 50% of their education—which is another persuasive reason to write the check for annual giving—or better, sign over that stock with the big capital gain!

It is very difficult to determine the cost per student in the traditional university accounting scheme. The problem is created by the twin missions of the university—teaching and research. Funds supporting both missions are like solids dissolving in a test tube. It would be unkind to suggest that the mixture is done purposely—but the consequences are purposeful. Research and instruction are quantitatively indistinguishable. What appears to be money spent on teaching undergraduates is money spent on research.

Faculty research is often an accounting charge allocated to instructional costs. The salary of an English professor on paid leave who is writing a book on a nineteenth century novelist is calculated as a part of undergraduate expenditures. The assumption is that researching and writing a book about a novelist makes a better teacher. Perhaps, but it would not be inappropriate for the published work to carry in its acknowledgments the appreciation that "this volume is brought to you with the partial support of undergraduate tuitions."

A teaching assistant doing exactly the same work as a tenured professor, but at a much lower price, reduces the per student cost of instruction. If it had not been possible to substitute teaching assistants to cover the reduced teaching load of professors, instructional costs would have become intolerable.

Undergraduates who have suffered in the classroom through the inexperience of teaching assistants, who themselves are learning the subject, and maybe the English language at the same time, will take no comfort in the irony that part of their tuition is subsidizing not only the on-leave tenured professor but the education of the graduate student.

* * *

Selecting a college or university is one of those decisions way up there—like who to marry, what kind of work to do, or whether to risk buying that house. Like buying a house, education is asset-building. It just seems more expensive because you can't do anything with it, like live in it. In a "middle-class melt," parents get the tuition bill and think of food stamps. The middle class feels squeezed between the deserving poor and the full-tuition rich.

Higher education has developed a sensible system for establishing eligibility for financial aid, though it's like dancing naked through the neighborhood. The family fills out a need analysis form. (The figures are confirmed by enclosing federal income tax returns.) Some factors used to evaluate eligibility are income, assets, family size, number attending college, and unusual expenses. The College Scholarship Service analyzes the information and makes an estimate of what the family can afford to pay. To boost the family contribution and reach the tuition price is an aid package worked out with the college consisting of gift aid (grants or scholarships), loans, and work-study. Getting meaningful facts about the quality of undergraduate education, and the costs assigned to it, are mandatory for making a judicious choice about where to apply and ultimately to matriculate.

11. EVALUATION & SOME FOLLIES

Clark Kerr, a respected guru of higher education, is probably right when he boasts that "the United States has, overall, the best system of higher education in the world. It provides more access, more diversity among its institutions (and thus more choice for prospective students), more service to the community, and better research and graduate training than anywhere else."

If more than its critics declare, and less than its defenders proclaim, colleges and universities do offer increasingly equal opportunities to enroll in institutions of choice. To be any good, the degrees achieved must be, and are, of unequal value in the economic and social marketplace. Higher education is a testament to America's belief in the equal right to become unequal. Decentralized, a mix of public and private, competitive for prestige within its varied clusters of similar academic cultures, the academy is the fertile womb of the American Dream.

Higher education, especially since World War II, has been a powerful individual-expanding force for an increasing percentage of the population. College redefines the identity of the self. It diminishes the ascribed characteristics of family background and gender. It expands the potential for individual achievement based on merit. College multiplies the already multitudinous options for working and living which are the gift of an advanced industrial society.

Why aren't prestigious private universities like the population of a town? The rich people live together and the less rich in descending scale in other parts of the town. A university does not obey the stratification customs of a town. Rich people don't attend the university with the highest tuition and in descending scale, like neighborhoods, the least rich enroll in institutions with the lowest tuition. While the rich are privileged, the access to private universities of meritorious young people is a testament to the faith in equal opportunity. To live in the better part of town is an expression of the right to be free; to earn the chance to live in the better part of town is made possible by equal access. What was a privilege before World War II became a right in 1944 with the G.I. Bill of Rights. The older prestigious universities responded to the egalitarian impulse by giving to merit the attention previously assigned to family background.

In the expansion of access to higher education, the most underreported and the least glamorous, as we have noted, are the community colleges. Along with the evening sessions of public and private universities, it is here that the sleepless immigrants go to begin their ascent. Higher education in the United States is superior to other countries in the opportunity to attend and in the diversity of different kinds of places to enroll. A greater percentage of the American population attends college than any other national population in the world. Colleges and universities serve their local communities with lectures and cultural events. More than half of all basic research carried forward in America is conducted on university campuses or affiliated institutes. Research in the humanities and the social sciences does produce its share of silly quests masquerading as profound investigations. A pontificality of professors does exchange incestuous banalities about inconsequential questions. In defense, what successful corporation is there which has not demonstrated its share of foolish failures?

Clark Kerr, in his proper boast about higher education, is strangely silent about two specific concerns of this analysis—the quality of undergraduate education and the cost effectiveness of universities. The self-reporting statistics tell us very little about what kind of a job universities are doing—a conclusion that may or may not be intended. On the quality of undergraduate education, most of the evidence is anecdotal. Most of that evidence consists of professors who sometimes engage in self-evaluation but more often fret about the quality of the freshman class. That is, blame it on the public school system. While 85% of public and 89% of private university faculties said they were very satisfied or satisfied with their autonomy and independence, 38% of public and 59% of the private university faculties complained about the quality of the students. Scores on admissions tests to graduate and professional schools is weak evidence, but what does exist is not good. Since the 1960s, scores on more than half of 24 graduate-school admissions tests have dropped.

One is tempted to echo the joke which used to make the rounds in Moscow:

Q: Have we really achieved full communism?

A: Not yet. Things are going to get a lot worse.

As the hunger for prestige through published research grows more ravenous, the quality of undergraduate education and the cost effectiveness of American universities is going to get worse.

"What we have on many campuses today is a crisis of purpose," asserted foundation executive Ernest Boyer in 1990. "Far too many colleges and universities are being driven . . . by the external imperatives of prestige. Even institutions that enroll primarily undergraduates—and have few if any resources for research—seek to imitate ranking research centers. . . . 'By believing themselves to be what they are not . . . ,' as Ernest Lynton and Sandra Elman of the University Massachusetts put it, 'institutions fall short of being what they could be.'"

Broader Leafage vs. Deeper Rootage

What could universities be? Well, the course offerings could be designed for the benefit of the students. Too often the courses offered are not what undergraduates should study but what the faculty wants to teach. This should not be a surprising observation. The faculty decide what is taught and who shall teach it. In the absence of positive incentives and negative regulatory pressures, why should professors decide in favor of the student rather than themselves when their self-interest, and the welfare of their dependent families, stand in conflict with student needs? The self-interest of professors lies in a correspondence between the subject to be taught and the subject of research. The more intimate the correspondence, the swifter the publication. Publications mean promotion to endowed chairs.

Since the subject of most scholarly articles and books is esoteric, taking such a course is like studying a tree without encompassing first the forest in which it is growing. Close examination of trees is rewarding for advanced undergraduates and graduate students. Freshmen and sophomores, most still teenagers in residential colleges, need first to locate themselves in the broader leafage of learning. Deeper rootage comes in the junior and senior years.

The curricular revolution following the 1960s is viewed by many as the disintegration of a learning core. Strict requirements in many institutions were relaxed. Students were no longer required to be familiar with a broad range of subject matter and specific methodologies. All learning is desirable, but courses are not all equal in their contribution to the intellectual growth of the student. Consumers on a limited budget recognize that buying a product means *not* buying something else. Students with limited spendable credits who are learning something in a course are always *not* learning something else in another course.

Less often noted is the lifting of restraints on the faculty. If students could go down the cafeteria line selecting from the curricular fare, faculty could expand the menu to courses which met *their* tastes. For professors bored by research, the new subject may simply be what they felt like talking about that year. The resulting academic meal did not represent a balanced intellectual diet for the average undergraduate. Still, universities that offered abundant course options gave their research faculty an advantage in the annual Bake-Off of papers at scholarly conventions.

A middle-aged reporter for the *New York Times* spent the spring of 1991 teaching at Colorado College, "a fine, small liberal arts school in the shadow of Pike's Peak." Some things had not changed since the time he began college in the 1950s, reported David Rosenbaum, like "the pervasive smell of stale beer on Sunday morning" or "the agony of acne." What had changed from his campus days was the curriculum: "Survey courses and prerequisites are passe. At Colorado College, no introductory course is offered in American history. Instead, freshmen and sophomores take narrower offerings like 'Women in America before the Civil War.' A history professor explained that no one on the faculty really wanted to teach introductory history and that, besides, students were assumed to have learned the fundamentals in high school. Students in other departments also take specialized courses without having had the basics. A sophomore English major said his introduction to Hemingway was a course this year devoted to how Hemingway novels deal with homosexuality."

On the graduate level professors teaching what they write about is generally beneficial for both graduate student and mentor. Doctoral candidates work as apprentices with practicing scholars, contributing to the mentor's research while watching how it is done. The mentors, however, do not so often encourage their protégés to write, as John Updike said of John Cheever, "as with a quill from the wing of an angel." Unfortunately, some drift off into their own world of knowing more and more about less and less. "He knew everything," recalled the widow about her scholar-husband, "but that's all he knew."

It's usually the maligned businessman who is scorned for pinched intellectual interests. The British observer Thomas Colley Grattan concluded long ago in 1859 that the mental capabilities of young American businessmen had been "cribbed into narrow limits. There is constant activity going on in one small portion of the brain; all the rest is stagnant. The money-making faculty is alone cultivated." That's certainly true, even today, of some businessmen; it also describes some scholars who have substituted for the "money-making faculty" a narrowly-focused obsession equally parochial in its limitations.

A liberal arts education is a journey into an expanded vision of life; the curriculum is the map that takes us there. Faculty specialization sabotages a liberal arts education. A narrow focus deflects teaching interests from those broad-gauged courses that engage comprehensive ideas through the study of events, thinkers, and artists in historical perspective. Freshmen and sophomores should engage issues explored in contrasting works in the humanities and revealed in events in the social sciences— free will vs. determinism, absolute vs. relative ethics, individual freedom vs. community obligations, ends vs. means.

A liberal arts education is wrestling with those messy, insoluble, cosmic issues that define who we are and what kind of society we have been and want to be—what is justice, how is beauty expressed, what is responsibility, are there different kinds of love, what is the good life? Those who came before—what have they to tell us? How can our intellectual experience take us together beyond ourselves into a deeper awareness for a richer life? Wisdom grows with an understanding of life's ironies and paradoxes, ambiguities and ambivalences. These are questions for generalists taking students on an adventure into contrasting texts and events, not specialists entering a tunnel of narrowing documents probing for answers to stunted questions.

Setting the More Goodly Human Powers in Motion

What a university could be is defined by what it is not. A university is not like the Human Resources division of a corporation. Corporations *instruct* their employees in data processing and salesmanship; universities *educate* undergraduates in the meaning of things. Corporations *train* their employees in skills; universities *transform* their students.

A university liberal arts education *transforms* the self. It sets the more goodly human powers in motion. It magnifies those qualities that we call admirable. Because universities move beyond information to transformation, they are charged with a special fiduciary responsibility. Universities are like a bank to which parents entrust their assets. In the more prestigious universities, presidents respond to the obligation by reminding their freshly minted graduates that the most important objective of their education has been the development of leadership qualities. Leadership—that's the objective of a college education. Be an achiever in the marketplace or a steward in public service. Best of all, try for both in a lifetime. The goal is to *do*, not *be*. The arena is work.

Universities could be an encounter with learning for the enjoyment of leisure. A college president justifying education for the purposes of leisure is no more likely than our Puritan forebears authorizing self-indulgence. The contentment of self-fulfilling leisure? The refinement of taste? Alas, no justification here for the life of the mind through books and art for their own sweet delight. No echo of a thought expressed by an appealing tradition in French painting—"Le fin de l'art est la délectation.—The goal of art is delight." Such pleasurable consequences in a pragmatic, egalitarian, faintly anti-intellectual society hint at the pretensions of the dilettante.

This is not to affirm that current academic expressions in literature and the arts offer delights easy to discern. It is sometimes hard to love it when the offerings are paintings without pictures, music without melody, novels without plots, and poetry without rhyme. Let others unkindly interpret current academic scab-picking as the egocentric pontificating of subsidized highbrows. There's always the past.

University leaders have found it difficult to resist the pragmatic demands of their society, but many never succumbed to the argument that the social sciences *deserved* the greater resources. Economics may prepare for work, and politics for the exercise of power, but the humanities shape the design of each. A nation's values are expressed in its literature and arts and philosophy—speculative stuff without much empirical verification. It's in the defining expressions of what is good and bad, right and wrong, ugly and beautiful that determine the destiny of a nation. Many leaders of major universities have never wavered from that conviction—however difficult a sell it may have been to certain members of the Board of Trustees.

* * *

Boards of Trustees are ultimately responsible for what a university is and could be. Trustees select the president and invest the portfolio of the endowment, though some boards do more. Most trustees and presidents get along very well together because they never lie to each other. The trustees tell the president what a great job he or she is doing. The president praises the board for the helpful reports submitted by its committees, especially the committee on grounds and buildings for its recent recommendation to save money by bulk purchases. With that in mind, and too often very little else, many trustees can be marked "present" with the rubber stamp of their mumbled "ayes."

Who cares to play the boat-rocking kill-joy at the quarterly trustee outing? The higher causes of truth-seeking and beauty-prizing are surcease from the wretched responsibilities of daily money-grubbing where a back turned is market share shaved. Trustees who interfere in educational matters are "meddlesome." In the housekeeping details for which business has trained many trustees, their advice is welcome and often followed. Universities are well managed in their physical plant and support services; they are badly managed in the utilization and the training of their human resources—the faculty.

Some Follies

Business executives stay competitive by incessantly pushing to improve quality and service while reducing costs. They do it by asking the right questions. What questions should parents, students, and alumni, executives, legislators, and taxpayers put to the campus of their choice? Four questions are follies—a waste of time however advantageous the reforms they propose may be. Their chances of acceptance are miniscule.

Why not a voucher plan? A voucher plan is generally thought of as a solution to the problems of public education. Each school-age child would receive a publicly funded entitlement worth a fixed amount of money. The parents select the school using the voucher to pay the tuition. For college-bound students, the freedom to choose seems even more suitable. One difference is that secondary school students are vouchered until they earn their high school diploma. The college voucher sustains its equity only so long as the student earns a passing grade. One advantage of the voucher plan on all educational levels would be to encourage Fortune 500 companies to think of education as a profit-making enterprise. For higher education, it's a plan ahead of its time.

Why not separate undergraduate colleges from huge state universities? Some state universities are so massive, with graduate programs and professional schools of law, medicine, business, theology, and engineering, that the scale is too big for a president and board of trustees to manage. The college of liberal arts for undergraduates would have its own president, board, budget, and faculty while sharing facilities with the professional schools. Better, move the entire undergraduate operation

117

to another location. For governors with such educational behemoths in their states, the proposal does not invite reelection.

Why not jettison tenure? How about substituting long-term contracts? Ten years is a sensible term. It's a fair way of increasing personnel flexibility while getting rid of ineffectual teachers. Arbitration would protect academic freedom—the professed justification for tenure. Professors already tenured would be exempt in a grandfather clause. The result would benefit everyone except the departing instructor who can't be very happy anyway knowing he is doing such a lousy job.

A threat to tenure is self-defeating and won't work. Prestigious colleges compete for scholars and proven scientists. What professor with a family to support is going to accept a long-term contract when a competing university will guarantee lifetime job security?

Change is unlikely when it defies institutional values. Change is possible when it reinforces those values or does not threaten them. The values that protect the hiring, promotion, and tenure systems are deeply embedded in the self-interest of the faculty. Those values also defend the paycheck security of the president and deans who are generally tenured professors in specific departments—the academy's companion to the golden parachute.

Revoking tenure is *very* difficult. Professor George Harker taught the concepts and philosophy of leisure. One of his projects was the study of nude beaches. What better way to view the philosophy of leisure? Professor Harker, however, was not fired for hanging out at nude beaches, but for gross professional incompetence. The Peoria, Illinois *Journal Star,* a local newspaper, was moved to grass-roots outrage: "The ordeal suffered by Western Illinois University leisure professor George Harker and by university officials who spent three years trying to fire him shows how far out of whack the university tenure system has become. Harker is the first teacher in the 92-year history of WIU [Western Illinois University] to be dismissed, and only the second in the 26-year history of the Board of Governors. Are we to believe that professors at the seven colleges which make up the BOG [Board of Governors] have all been so good at what they do that no one ever considered getting rid of them? We doubt it. It took five months of hearings, 1,400 pages of testimony and more than $35,000 in legal fees—to date—to fire Harker. No wonder no one ever gets fired!"

However grossly self-serving tenure has become, in a world where job insecurity seems on the increase, one is reminded of Cicero's observation: "We are in bondage to the law so that we may be free." Tenure was established in the early decades of the twentieth century essentially to protect faculty from vengeful trustees with differing political viewpoints. Who would have thought then that now tenure might be used to protect professors, not from trustees or politicians or the public, but from students charging racism, sexism, or ethnicism, especially WASPism. The bondage of tenure at least encourages professors to think without fear—which is the price that probably must be paid for so much foolish thinking.

Why not improve undergraduate teaching by weighing more heavily the criterion of teaching effectiveness in the granting of tenure? Foundation executives, attended by invited university administrators, periodically conjoin in order to lament how "publish or perish" continues to dominate promotion judgments. (Perishing from publishing is not pondered.)

The promotion-through-teaching recommendation has become one of those exhortations that can be so comforting to task forces on higher education. The members of the task force gather in worried counsel, discuss and accept the recommendation, justify their fee by voting unanimously for it, and go home. The chance of persuading university faculties is zip—and it's the faculty that initiates promotion recommendations. The reason is simple. Scholars want to be a member of a department with a national reputation for research. (Not welcome in the department are competitors in the professor's specialty.) Popular teachers do nothing to enhance the distinction of the department. Popular teachers may play big in the student newspaper, but Mr. Chips doesn't get reviewed in the international journals. Indeed, "popular" is not an accolade that resonates pleasantly in the academic ear. Popular novelists, poets, and composers can't be good if the public likes them. Teachers who are too popular are suspect for the same reason.

Presidents, deans, and trustees, alas, speak with forked tongue. They call for more recognition of good teaching with prizes and salary incentives. The reality is closer to the experience of Harvard University's distinguished paleontologist, Stephen Jay Gould: "To be perfectly honest, though lip service is given to teaching, I have never seriously heard teaching considered in any meeting for promotion. . . . Writing is the currency of prestige and promotion."

An academic budget is a zero-sum game. For every winner, there must be a loser. It's like sports or politics. There are winners who score the most points or get the most votes—and there are losers. To promote a dazzling teacher is to lose a promising scholar. The choice is not always so boldly differentiated. But it's *always* a matter of degree. When the tilt is in favor of the candidate who prefers teaching to published research, the slide of the university into a less prestigious rank is set in motion. So, presidents must endure the duplicity of promoting in public the qualities of teachers whom they cannot promote in private. The teacher-scholar ideal has always been a valiant effort to deny the zero-sum uncharitableness of faculty promotion.

12. DOABLES—IMPROVE QUALITY

Politics is the art of the deliverable. That art is tested daily when power is spread through a spiderweb of collegial governance. Buzzing about with threatening proposals can result in being captured and eaten at a committee meeting.

Change in universities will not come from within but from without. Outside reformers will wisely follow management consultant Peter Drucker's advice: "Don't solve problems. Pursue opportunities." Problems are embedded in the self-interest of faculty which is the power source of the university. Opportunities may challenge the power source but to be effective must not threaten it.

Working comfortably within the system means conceding the truism affirmed by a professor at a top research university: "Only a few institutions can maintain a quality research reputation and a quality instructional program. In most, one comes at the expense of the other. . . ." *Nothing proposed here is at the expense of achieving and sustaining a quality research reputation. That mission remains primary.* While the reforms do not undermine academic distinction through published research, neither do they threaten the faculty. If they did, like the four follies in the previous chapter, they would be doomed. At the same time, it must be confessed that there is no expectation of certain professors, and on each campus they know who they are, greeting the arrival of this tome with high-fives!

* * *

How to achieve better undergraduate teaching and a more cost-effective university? The questions to be raised, and the reforms proposed, all touch upon the faculty. The faculty is the most important force in a university. It is the teacher in a sacred classroom who ignites the torch of learning. It's that torch illuminating the lives of students which is what teaching is all about.

The seven queries, and the reforms that emerge from them, all address a subject that businessmen did not confront with watchful regu-

121

larity—until foreign competition threatened. They do now. It's productivity. Educational productivity is the relation of effectiveness to costs. The first query begins with getting numbers that have meaning for student costs and faculty productivity.

Three questions touch upon the relationship of faculty to undergraduates. One probes for ways of getting rid of incompetent teachers without violating the sanctity of tenure. Another asks what is being done to improve the quality of undergraduate teaching. A third asks if there is a faculty development program.

The faculty is also the costliest item in the budget. It is the most sensible place to begin asking questions about reducing costs. The focus shifts from the quality of performance to the quantity of time. How much time is spent in consensus decision making on administrative matters? How can faculty time be put to better use by the increasing use of technology? How does each member of the faculty spend his or her work time and with what kind of measurable results?

Demand Meaningful Accounting

University accounting practices used to be about as lively a subject for discussion as last year's commencement address. Then, in 1991, Stanford University's president, Donald Kennedy, agreed before a House subcommittee that Stanford had overcharged the Federal Government for indirect research costs. The government was billed for the costs of operating a 72-foot yacht, a $4,000 wedding reception at the president's house, enlargement of the president's bed, $7,000 for sheets, $400 for flowers for a dedication of the school's stables, and a lot more. The Stanford probe triggered a widespread investigation of how universities were overcharging the government for indirect (overhead) costs associated with research. Like penitents confessing their sins, universities under investigation began to reimburse or withdraw overhead charges—membership dues for a country club, a trustees retreat, a retirement dinner, air fare to the Caribbean for a president's wife. At issue, too, were the differences in percentage figures for indirect (overhead) costs imposed on the direct costs. Some universities charged over 80% and others less than 50%. It was all very embarrassing.

It was also humiliating. John Dingell, chairman of the House Energy and Commerce Committee, as well as the subcommittee on oversight and investigations, talked in terms of corrupt military contractors and inside traders. "Our purpose," he explained, "is simply to compel universities and scientists to clean up their act and to see to it that public money is properly spent." Dingell was no kinder to the groves of academe than to Wall St. "It's a closed world," he said of the academic establishment, "in which the inhabitants are fiercely protective of their world, of themselves and of each other, and where intruders are poorly treated at best."

Stanford's chief financial officer saw it differently. "We thought we were doing the public good," explained William Massy. "We didn't think of ourselves as a defense contractor. That was a profit-making enterprise—lots of perks. We were serving the public interest, not private interests." Paul Biddle, the Navy official responsible for overseeing federal research on the campus and the one who finally blew the whistle, allowed as how "it was outright greed for noble purposes."

Former Secretary of Education William Bennett was having none of that argument: "The more that comes to light about the behavior of some of our more prestigious universities, the more one sees that their posture of moral superiority is not merited. These are places that are holier than thou telling the Government how to act, and now here are charges of good old-fashioned corruption."

Bennett's charge may be a bit harsh, but it does suggest the problem of reforming the university. The assumption of moral superiority is confirmed by Paul Biddle's excuse that at Stanford "it was outright greed for noble purposes." Presumably, research in pursuit of truth is nobler than research in pursuit of profit. The purity of truth's goal somehow diminishes the stain of unethical means. The same for undergraduate education. How can anyone devoted to such a noble cause behave in a way that is less than noble? Is not the pursuit of the goal proof of the quality of the pursuer?

Asking questions leading to *meaningful accounting of university numbers about money allocated to undergraduate instruction and how the faculty spends its time* may confront a resisting moral posture. The Congress, of course, enjoys the power of subpoena. Since the Federal Government currently pays over 9 billion dollars a year to higher education for research and provides some 12 billion dollars in student aid, the magnitude of Congressional fiduciary responsibility is greater than a lone citizen requesting numbers at the local university. But it's only a matter of degree.

Encourage Early Retirement

Early retirement is used increasingly in business. In the academy, unlike business, early retirement is not a coercive personnel instrument. It cannot be used to compel the retirement of a tenured professor. At the same time, heart-to-hearts between the faltering teacher and the departmental chairperson, consultations with the appropriate dean, and informal sessions with the president can over the period of a year or two introduce the attractions of a surcease from those labors that have lost the enchantment that fortified the young preceptor long ago. The "golden handshake" can be made more agreeable by financial enticements and more comforting by professional counseling. The dispatch of early retirement for the fatigued in mind and spirit becomes a blessing for students forced to bear the teacher's ennui.

Paying for an early retirement requires a trade-off. The responsible dean may in this case ethically give way to the temptation of hiring cheaper labor to do the same job. As we explained earlier, 30-year-old assistant professors do much the same kind of work as expensive 60-year-old full professors.

Require Teacher Training

The irony is that universities, which are assigned the responsibility of education, fail to help their teachers be good teachers while major corporations, which are assigned other responsibilities, spend huge sums teaching executives how to be effective executives. Manufacturers were bullied into executive training by Japanese competition. The university lacks a bully.

How much training of teachers is there in universities? Young instructors just starting out receive little guidance from either peers or senior faculty. You learn to teach by self-teaching. Graduate school is no help. It is designed to produce scholars. Teachers are apparently supposed to know how to teach because they have been watching teachers do it since first grade—kind of like learning how to play tennis by sitting in a grandstand.

One problem in the academy is that the punishment-reward nexus is very weak. Tenured professors are required to show up for class, transact the instructional rituals, and behave themselves morally. But there is no way to force them to improve their competence in teaching, e.g., like threatening the axe. How can you punish tenured professors? Take away their parking places? Schedule their classes at 8:00 o'clock Monday morning? Cut their family from the invitation list for the Christmas party at the president's mansion? It's all pretty much wrist-slapping.

Neither are the campus rewards potent. The Carnegie Foundation for the Advancement of Teaching surveyed colleges and universities and concluded that "on too many campuses, teaching frequently is not well rewarded, and especially for young professors seeking tenure, it's much safer to present a paper at a national convention than it is to spend time with undergraduates back home."

The reward for good teaching is the applause of the students. At the faculty club that kind of recognition would probably kindle dangerous distrust rather than admiring emulation, more likely arouse suspicions about catering to capricious adolescents than create respect for perfecting a craft. For the accomplished teacher on the lecture platform, student applause, alas, cannot be translated into dollars or into print. Student applause is ephemeral—measured in minutes. In contrast, the print of published research is forever. A book is the scholar's immortality.

Hey, how about another prize for good teaching? In business, the motion recalls the gesture of a bigger plaque for the guy who did such a great job raising money in this year's United Way campaign!

* * *

Over the past decade, sensible CEOs have put the weight of their authority behind management training. Teacher training, the equivalent of management training, has yet to fertilize the groves of academe. Most universities continue to ignore systematic training that would improve the quality of teaching.

The strategy must create a campus culture that praises rather than ignores the teacher *who wants to improve.* Without a full-court press from the president, deans, and departmental chairpersons, the drive towards teacher improvement will falter about the same time the inspirational memo hits the rim of the wastebasket.

Systematic teacher training of tenured faculty will require massive buttressing, more than likely from trustee support. Teacher training raises suspicions about the ideal of the teacher-scholar. That ideal was crucial for the successful modification of the British tradition of a teaching college to the German model of a research institution. *Universities had to prove that what they were doing they were not doing.* What they were doing was shifting the university from chiefly teaching to primarily research. To prove they were *not* doing that, they claimed that the promising scholars promoted to tenure were really good teachers. Thus were the education of undergraduates and the gaining of scholarly prestige attended to with equal fidelity.

University presidents and deans kept polishing the image of the teacher-scholar ideal. Representative viewpoints from college administrators allow for little qualification:

It is impossible to separate effective teaching from research.

I take issue with the idea that really effective teaching can be done by men who are not engaged in research.

The really distinguished men in research are almost always good teachers.

It is difficult, if not impossible, to find an instance of a great undergraduate teacher who was not a vigorous investigator and critic. . . .

The transition to the research university took place during the latter part of the nineteenth and the first half of the twentieth centuries. Presidents of universities, along with the clergy, were the moral leaders of their time, not just another special interest group. Presidents of prestigious universities were accountable for shaping the characters (and the minds) of their students just as the clergy were charged with saving the souls of their parishioners. The students at prestigious universities were not just any students but the children of other national leaders.

It would be unfair to accuse the leaders of higher education of fraud. They were striving to remain faithful to an earlier heritage of teaching while embracing another mission. The delusion that made morally bearable the shift to a research objective was the promotion of the teacher-scholar ideal. It was not a conspiracy but a masquerade. Most believed what was behind the mask—except for the usual maverick who always feels compelled to prick the balloon of institutional rationalization.

The maverick was Edmund Ezra Day, the president of Cornell. His deflating message was a 1939 address to the powerful Association of American Universities. "Teaching and research are not experiencing equal favor . . . ," Day lectured his colleagues. "One of the comfortable ways of dealing administratively with this situation is to belittle the idea that teaching and research are in any way competing functions at the university level. The idea is that teaching and research go hand in hand; that the successful teacher will inevitably be engaged in fruitful research; and the successful scholar or scientist just as surely will be an effective teacher. This proposition in this general form is wishful thinking of the baldest sort. The eminent scholar or scientist who is also an inspiring teacher is, of course, for the university administrator an answer to prayer; but we know all too well that answers to this particular prayer appear in the flesh *very infrequently."*

Indeed, one could argue that teaching and research are not mutually reinforcing but incompatible. It may even take different personality types to do one or the other with excellence, though there are a rare few who can do both with brilliance. More certainly, during the school year time for undergraduates and attention to research are in daily competition for the energies of productive professors.

Anton Chekhov was both a physician and a playwright. "Medicine is my lawful wife, literature my illegitimate spouse," he confessed. "Of course, they interfere with each other, but not so much as to exclude each other." Chekhov's facility in reconciling competing loyalties is seldom emulated in the academy. Teaching and research, wife and mistress, cannot so easily be conciliated by professors desirous of satisfying both pleasures with equal fidelity.

Teaching and research are fit toil for lively minds. The tasks, however, take the professor in different directions. Teaching demands breadth of learning while research forces a narrowing into expertise. As we suggested earlier, scholarly specialization requires intensely cultivating an ever-smaller corner of the subject matter field while neglecting the broader expanse.

There is no more correspondence between an eminent scholar and a superior teacher than between a brilliant theologian and an inspiring preacher. In building their prestigious universities, presidents and deans believed in the ideal of the teacher-scholar and invoked it as a justification for promoting scholars to tenure. They still do. Thus is a life with delusions intolerable, but a life without delusions morally unbearable.

Fortunate alumni will recall that rare exception of the caring teacher within the renowned scholar and cherish the memory. The evidence, however, confirms as fantasy the ideal of the predominate teacher-scholar. After reviewing the empirical research, Martin Finkelstein discovered: "That good research is both a necessary and sufficient condition for good teaching . . . is not resoundingly supported by the evidence." Harold Yuker also reviewed the evidence and concluded: "No relationship is apparent . . . between scholarly publications and teaching effectiveness."

Faculty and students evaluate differently the connection between research competence and teaching effectiveness. Faculty prefer intellectual substance as the criterion for measuring teaching quality and see a closer connection between research activity and good teaching. Students stress the personality of the teacher and for them "the expertise developed via research activity appears a largely irrelevant factor." It is not surprising that faculty emphasize *what* is presented while students value *how* it is presented. It's the students who spend the semester listening.

A probe into just how teaching competence is evaluated is going to be embarrassing. What is there beyond student evaluations? "It's extremely rare, in my experience," reports Vanderbilt University's Chester Finn, Jr., "for fellow professors, department chairmen, deans, or provosts actually to observe anyone in the classroom. On most campuses, such an appearance would be cause for anxiety, suspicion, and much muttering. Hence any assessment of one's teaching by one's colleagues is apt to be based on vague general impressions, on hearsay, and on student comments."

Public schools are always being told by colleges how much the colleges can help them do a better job. Teacher training is one activity in which the public schools can teach the colleges a thing or two. The better school systems have adopted proven training programs that use techniques ranging from videotape replays through student feedback to role playing in order to help teachers overcome everything from annoying speaking habits to sloppy presentations. To show how teaching is theater is not to reduce the craft to a soap opera but rather elevate the privilege to an art form.

* * *

The good news is that the bad news about why undergraduate teaching is not better is becoming news. The *Chronicle of Higher Education* reported in 1989 that "at large universities, teaching assistants may be responsible for teaching 25 per cent of undergraduate classes, or an even bigger proportion." The statistics on the training of these *teaching assistants* is appalling. Only 25% of institutions using teaching assistants have campus-wide training programs. Of those who do field such programs, only half require participation. In the academic departments, only half provide training for teaching assistants. Most offer little follow-up.

The amount of training for *tenured professors* is mostly committee talk and task force verbiage. Reality is on the level of the president's declaration that teaching this year is going to be weighed more heavily in the promotion to tenure. Edmund Ezra Day again spoke to the point in historical perspective: "On every campus we encounter the theory which many professors find strangely reassuring, that teaching is a mysterious art, the essence of which can never be known. . . . Nevertheless, teaching, like other forms of professional practice, is susceptible to analysis, and the essentials of good teaching are generally recognized, even if efforts to discover their concrete existence in the work of any university faculty are strongly resisted." That was a half century ago, and there have been some changes in research universities. More professors receive released time from teaching to investigate how a program can be initiated. The question to ask of those programs in existence, designed to improve the teaching effectiveness of tenured faculty, is: What percentage of the faculty participate and with what intensity? Still, in all fairness, many university administrators do seem at last to be getting the message and are forcing the faculty to confront the problem.

As in business, the boss' support is key to a successful training program. Presidents must verify that the initiative is top priority and not lip service. They must invoke the values of respect for self-development and pride in a job well done. They must personally acknowledge improvement. Departmental chairpersons should persuade all members of the department, as a matter of institutional loyalty, to participate in the training program. The amount of time each professor spends with the trainer is confidential. For that, and other reasons, it is better to begin by subcontracting the operation.

Teacher training costs money, like switching the clerical staff from typewriters to word processing. The difference is that foundations are eager to respond with start-up funding for programs that address the issue of instructional improvement. The traditional approach is to call for teaching as a more heavily weighted criterion for promotion to tenure. That approach, as we have suggested, is not promising. A more viable strategy is invoking what the president and deans are supposed to be there for—leadership. Responsible leaders will find ways to encourage the faculty to use a training program when discreet facilities and sensitive trainers are made available. Sturdy support from trustees is a *sine qua non* to combat faculty defiance.

Encourage Growth Compacts

A major contribution to corporate culture has been the addition of the human resources division. It used to be called "personnel." That's where secretaries were hired, and as fringe benefits evolved, health insurance and pensions were explained.

The office of personnel graduated to the division of human resources as human resources replaced natural resources as the wealth-producing variable in international economic competition. People became more precious as their skills became more valuable. Evaluation under older procedures was solely designed to measure employee performance. Evaluation has stretched into an exchange. Employee and employer set the goals. Together they design ways to achieve the goals with timetables to stay on schedule and training programs to enhance personal qualifications.

University culture has pretty much ignored human resources practices with respect to their biggest cost center. The paperwork between faculty and employer has become more regulated and more voluminous over the past half century. But tenured or no, after earning the doctorate, professors are on their own for the rest of their professional lives. As we have suggested, they receive plenty of critical feedback from scholarly journals, publishers, and reviewers. Very little help in their teaching. Generally none at all in their professional development.

With such a massive and irrevocable lifetime commitment, it is reasonable to assume that universities would have structured some formal mechanism for nurturing professors who were faltering in their teaching or research. There is, of course, the annual report to the departmental chairperson. It is a factual statement of the past year's activities. The requirement is not an exchange. It offers no encouragement for self-development, no counseling for ways to improve relations with students, no psychic support for breaking through blocks to resume once again serious scholarship.

What might be called "growth compacts" would emerge from scheduled sessions with the teacher/scholar. Growth compacts ("contracts" sounds too legal) are a synergy of skill training, goals setting, evaluation, and psychotherapy. One objective might be getting that book done. Another might acknowledge, after years of denial, the insulting evaluations by students of classroom performance with a program to do something about it. In each case, the target would be results to be achieved by agreed goals, doable means, and specific timetables.

* * *

Every university faculty is a tragedy of wasted resources. So many who entered the profession to teach must do everything they can to get out of it. A reduced teaching load is a testament of faith in the teacher's scholarly promise. The Carnegie Foundation for the Advancement of Teaching conducted surveys that expose the irony: Over 70% of professors say their interest lies primarily in teaching. More specifically for our purposes, 33% of the faculty in "research universities" are primarily interested in teaching while 55% of the faculty in other "doctorate-granting" universities profess that interest. In our university prototype, it is safe to say that a healthy percentage of the 33% and 55% just love to teach and prefer teaching to the lonely scholar's study.

When a university is getting started, it's like wet cement that can be shaped to design objectives. When universities get old, and most are old, the cement of custom has hardened. To crack that cement and introduce *growth compacts in teaching* requires the jackhammer of *mandatory, systematic, written procedures*.

The beginning is *self-assessment.* If the unexamined life is not worth living, the teaching life of most professors is so unexamined as to be brain-dead. To introduce a course in most universities, some kind of syllabus is required, i.e., what the course is about, what are the readings, why should it be added to the curriculum. Rarely is the professor required to write a postmortem that would ask: How can I do this better the next time?

Peer evaluation is useful but makes everyone uncomfortable. The person who needs the most help is usually the most defensive. For the peer pressured into observing a colleague, evaluation consumes a lot of time, particularly if the objective is to improve performance rather than simply criticize. The interaction is emotionally draining. It takes the finesse of a theatrical director and the resourcefulness of an athletic coach. The people who do it best are the people trained as professionals. Using the instant replay features of videotaping or discerning psychological hang-ups is not a task for amateurs.

Student evaluation of teaching proves the wisdom of the maxim: It is not permitted in the most equitable of persons to be a judge in their own cause. Student assessments are most useful when combined with a comprehensive approach to teaching improvement. The teacher who gets a flunking grade is like a wounded deer staring into the headlights of an onrushing automobile. That's about where most universities leave their wounded faculty.

Student evaluation of teaching lists compliments and complaints. The process should be more than that. It should be a creative contribu-

131

tion to the learning process. The traditional approach requires, or asks, students to fill out a form ranking faculty performance. A more rewarding proceeding follows the advice of current management principles: Pay attention to the customer and listen to the worker. In this felicitous case, the customer and the worker are the same. The student buys the credits towards a degree and does the work to earn them. Factories call worker-feedback "quality circles." In the academy, they are known as "student review teams." The teams join the teacher in a collaborative effort to produce a better product. A professor, guaranteed an income for life, with stale mind reading in monotone from dusty notes, will ignore the howl of "no's" to the evaluation query: "Would you advise your best friend to take this course?" Jump-starting that mind with the booster cables of student input (paid for in credits or money) may do some good. It's a sound investment in student learning and teacher training.

Alumni evaluation is rare but is obviously very revealing. Alumni who think back for a moment can recall a teacher whom they have come to value more highly after graduation. Mailed forms to alumni, perhaps as part of the fifth-year reunion, would ask not only for evaluations of professors but an assessment of their own educational experience. While the development office will counsel against provoking bad vibes, the alumni might surprise the university with an increase in annual giving. You mean they are actually conducting a consumer survey—in addition to banging the tin cup?

Teaching is a precious act. Responsible adults do it with a natural reverence. Universities smother that reverence with rewards for research, lesser rewards for good teaching, and few punishments for bad teaching. Why should professors behave any differently from anyone else in similar circumstances? Growth compacts don't fight losing battles but work within the system. They offer universities some time to enter the twentieth century of human resources management—before the twenty-first century gets here.

13. DOABLES—CUT COSTS

Time has no value except in its use. In business, "time is money." The productive use of time increases wealth. In the academy, time is crucial because the costs are in labor rather than materials. Productivity is measured by the effective use of faculty time in teaching, research, and administrative tasks. We begin with one administrative task.

Modify Peer Review

Sacred to the spirit of the university is the faith in faculty self-governance. Faculty self-governance has its most profound consequences in the peer review of appointment, promotion, and tenure. The usual procedure is for departments to initiate and the administration to veto. Observers might ask: Why not the reverse for tenure appointments? The president, provost, and deans initiate, in consultation with the department, while the peer review of the department vetoes?

The nomination by the administration of candidates for tenure, checked by departmental review, has at least four advantages. First, it fixes accountability. In the collegial process, responsibility is shared by peers with minimal supervision from above. Accountability cannot be assigned if it is not known who votes for whom in the departmental meeting. While it may be important for morale to praise, detecting blame in an organization is crucial. Trustees cannot hold presidents accountable for performance without guaranteeing them the authority for decision making. Who can blame the coach for a losing season when the players are granted the authority to select the quarterback?

Second, administrative origination of tenure appointments is more objective. The tenure criteria of scholarship, teaching, and campus/community contributions are established and ranked. Evaluations of candidates are recorded in their folders. With the criteria agreed upon and the evaluations of each candidate recorded in writing, including outside assessments, is it not unreasonable to ask why professors in a departmental meeting are any more or less qualified to judge the evidence than the dean, provost, and president? For certain, if the administration initiates the tenure nomination, the risk of subjective personal preferences in the department is reduced. Undermined is the professor who could block the bringing forward of a name from another university because the candidate might compete for choice graduate students or a coveted endowed chair.

Third, the shift of authority reinforces control over strategic planning. To what fields should the university allocate resources? What are the projections for student course selections, for significant areas of research? What departments are locking the university into an inflexible posture with too many tenured positions?

Fourth, the proposal saves time. Collegial decision making is extraordinarily time-consuming. Professors constantly growl that committees are time-wasting. After more than forty years in academia, Murray Rothbard came to the conclusion that in a typical departmental or faculty meeting "the intensity of discussion and debate is inversely proportional to the importance of the topic. . . ." The irony, of course, is that the faculty complains about what they have brought upon themselves. If *representative* democracy encourages the growth of committees, how many more and bigger committees are required when *direct* democracy is the structure for decision-making, i.e., when every professor is his or her own legislator. When the faculty administrates, professors rob students and research projects of energies they were primarily employed to use for teaching and scholarship.

Finally, administrative proposing of tenure candidates with departmental review is simply more humane. Ever had lunch with a guy for five years and then been asked to banish him and his family? Ever voted for a colleague's candidate with the implied understanding that next time he would vote for the assistant professor for whom you have been playing the admired mentor? Tenure judgments are meant to be objective; they are too often subjective decisions.

* * *

An innocent reporter asked Woodrow Wilson what it was like giving up the serene campus of Princeton University for the governorship of New Jersey. How did he handle the rough-n'-tumble of state politics? "I don't want you to suppose that when I was nominated for Governor of New Jersey I emerged from academic seclusion, where nothing was known of politics . . . ," explained the then Governor of New Jersey, former university president, and future President of the United States.

"I'll confide in you as I have already confided to others—that, as compared with the college politician, the real article seems like an amateur."

Politics is the exercise of power to have your own way—which is what most of us have wanted since we were kids. It's harsh enough in business and the fee-based professions. In universities, politics has a particularly bad name. "What has for years been said about academic politics most certainly can be said about literary politics as well," reported the columnist Jonathan Yardley. "Why is it so vicious? Because the stakes are so small." The viciousness may also be a consequence of the way decisions are made. In business, judgments about the career destiny of executives are made by superiors. In universities, personnel decisions are made by peers. If academic politics is accused of being petty, nasty, and often vicious, it's not because of the nature of professors—though some critics are wont to make that unfair charge. It may indeed be the size of the stakes. But it's also because members of a faculty are asked to sit in judgment on their friends and enemies. To require professors to sit as jurors and render a verdict on one of their own is to force them to be political with each other. Further, to lose by a collegial vote of peers is more hurtful than to be banished by a single boss. The boss is another person; the peers are oneself judging oneself. Peer review encourages swelling egos where judicious restraint should rule, emotion where reason should prevail.

It may be that peer review is so sacrosanct because the tenured faculty arrived there by the process. How could something so right be wrong? Many breadwinners in other industries, however, arrived at their responsibilities by a different process and may bring to the exploration of peer review a contrasting perspective.

Use Technology

What kinds of technology have been sluggishly accepted by professors? The kind that reproduces other professors teaching a similar course.

Higher education has been quick to adopt some technological innovations. Public address systems make it easier to hear, overhead projectors make it easier to see, and photographic slides projected onto a screen make it easier to visualize—and all require a live person to be the controlling focus of student attention. Incorporated with alacrity were examinations that machine-graded students. Filling in the correct bubble with a stubby No. 2 pencil, rather than writing an essay in response to a provocative question, is easier for both student and teacher. Slow to find acceptance has been the use of videotapes that reproduce another teacher giving similar lectures or presenting standard laboratory demonstrations.

"If you don't teach live, you're dead," sounds like a maxim, but it's a Luddite fallacy. Hi-tech does not diminish the need for workers; it changes the way workers do their work. A videotape of a master teacher in biology can play endlessly the sequence of dissecting a frog. The student in self-pacing confidence can repeatedly view a troublesome maneuver. What the teacher on the videotape cannot do is interact with a student in the one-to-one adventure of discovery. The on-site teacher, who once had to strain to keep fresh the exercise in a demonstration lecture, can now move about the laboratory offering hi-touch attention to individual students.

A course on the history of Western civilization is now available on 52 half-hour videotapes. The cultivated lecturer, Eugen Weber of the University of California at Los Angeles, enriches the spoken text with visuals dramatizing the historical narrative of the Western tradition. The professor on campus who once lectured the course is now free to work with students interactively—analyzing readings in discussion groups and sharpening student writing skills with editorial critiques.

Technology threatens the ego of the teacher. Just as there was no music until the listener could see the bow and the fiddle together, so there was no learning for great numbers until a teacher lectured to students. Gutenberg changed that forever. Continuing the trend are inexpensive paperback books, duplicating machines, computers, videotapes, and recently videodisks.

The lecturing spigot flowing into passive student sponges is as pedagogically enlightened as turning schoolchildren loose in New York City during the summer months to help with the planting and harvesting. Lecturing persists in universities as the favorite format of learning—overwhelmingly. Asked to describe the most recent class session they held in an undergraduate course, 7% of the university professors said they lectured continuously; 73% lectured for most of the period, pausing now and then for student questions or comments; 9% said they lectured for perhaps 15 or 25 minutes but not during the rest of the period; while 11% said that for the most part they had done "something else." Continuous teacher talk offers students one advantage. They can skip the lecture and buy the notes from a professional notetaker.

Unlike lecturing, technology shifts the focus from the self of the teacher to the screen of the television set and the monitor of the computer. Replacement technology dethrones the teacher. Students are no longer dependent on the older and wiser resource. Replacement technology intimidates justifications for existence.

The inquirer must probe here with caution. Technology is often perceived as a threat to job security. Finding ways to inquire about the faculty doing a cheaper, better job without threatening no job will summon a full measure of tact. Remember that no technological innovation is ever introduced into a university classroom without faculty support. Approval is insufficient. The faculty may approve; each professor decides individually the degree of implementation.

Mandate Differential Faculty Workloads

Finally, the campus visitor, sheltered by virginal innocence, will be forgiven when inquiring: "How does the faculty spend its time?" It's the key question for productivity analysis. The answers have consequences for the national interest. "The U.S. college industry lives in a comfortable marketplace, largely isolated from price competition and with little constraint on inefficiencies," declared staff writer Leslie Spencer of *Forbes*, adding ominously, "So did the U.S. automobile industry only a few decades ago." Columnist Robert J. Samuelson of *Newsweek* was blunt: Higher education is "hugely wasteful."

Faculty workloads, or "the load" as it is often called, measures one of the three professorial responsibilities—teaching. The measuring instrument is crude. The teaching load is calculated by the number of hours spent teaching in a classroom. Hours can also be awarded for specific numbers of undergraduates, masters, and doctoral candidates who work with the professor on the students' research projects. Sometimes committee work and special administrative assignments are credited to the workload. For example, a senior professor may regularly teach six hours in the fall (two courses) and nine hours in the spring (three courses). A laborious committee assignment over the academic year might be counted the equivalent of one course, so in the spring the load would be nine hours but two courses (six hours) would be taught. When teaching undergraduates is converted to other responsibilities (including sometimes research), the result is called a "reduced load" or "released time." Most committee assignments, however, as well as faculty self-governance and peer review, are part of the job. The professor is expected to hold office hours at stated times each week.

The more colleges push to become universities and the more universities strain for scholarly prestige, the fewer students taught by the faculty and the less productivity per student. The less productivity per student, the higher the cost to nourish the undergraduate to the baccalaureate. The higher the cost, the higher the tuition. Robert V. Iosue, the president of York College in Pennsylvania, put the sequence in historical perspective in 1987 for the readers of the *Wall Street Journal*: "A few decades ago professors taught 15 credits a semester (about one-half the teaching load of a high-school teacher today) and were expected to engage in research. Today, some teach 12 credits, but nine credits is the norm at many colleges. In my own state of Pennsylvania, we have a large number of two-year public colleges at which the teaching load is only nine credits a semester; these schools have virtually no research facilities."

Iosue, virtually alone among his kind in the sanctum of academic presidents, does not make life any easier for his fundraising colleagues. He continues the faultfinding: "We have substantially reduced teaching loads so that we can engage in scholarship and remain active in our fields. But to imply that all 500,000 of our full-time faculty are engaged in research is to challenge credulity. Even to suppose that those teaching only nine credits are engaged in significant research is a grievous error. . . . We seem to feel that because a few faculty engage in research, all faculty do so. . . . that because a few faculty need to teach less in order to do research, all faculty need to teach less."

The evidence supports Iosue. Some 50 percent of faculty at research and doctorate-granting universities have never published or edited a book or monograph. The educational consultant Jay Amberg, writing for the *American Scholar*, concluded that "few professors are significantly involved in research. One ballpark estimate holds that 80 percent of the research is being done by 10 percent of the faculty at 20 percent of the universities."

Some professors claim that if their workload was reduced, they would publish their research. Harold Yuker reviewed the studies on workloads and found that "reduced load usually does not result in increased research productivity. . . . Decreasing the load of nonproductive faculty members seldom results in scholarly productivity. . . . It is probable that if teaching loads were reduced, faculty members would either devote more time to activities other than research or reduce their total work week. . . . At every institution, in every department, and in every rank, some faculty members work fewer than 30 hours a week while others work more than 70."

If productive scholarship cannot be cultivated by teaching fewer hours in the classroom, we should probably acknowledge temperament more than brains. As a professor said of his departmental colleague— "Every time Charlie sights the glimmering of an idea, he feels compelled to print it for the edification of his peers." Partly it's being born that way and partly conditioning. How explain the budding career of a youngster, not yet enrolled in the first grade, who was destined to become a great historian. His mother asked him one late night why he was not asleep and he replied: "I'm lying awake thinking about the past."

Sage inquirers, trying to determine the number of hours professors actually spend with undergraduates in the classroom, should ask about released time (reduced load) for other assigned responsibilities. Also, an hour is not like a one hour meeting in business. A contact hour in the classroom is 50 minutes, so a six-hour teaching load per week is really five hours of instruction.

What might be called credit inflation sometimes distorts the calculation. One hour in the classroom is usually one credit. Sometimes four credits are given for three hours in the classroom for reasons that are not always persuasive. One hesitates to be indelicate, but self-reported statistics are not always as precise as they might be. On-site audits are advisable.

* * *

Identical faculty workloads measured in classroom teaching hours are not *equal* faculty workloads measured by the nature of the teaching, the kinds of administrative campus duties, service to the community, and tangible research. A more precise measurement of faculty time is required to initiate the process of accountability. The measurement might be called *productivity units.* Productivity units measure the *teaching* function of the faculty workload by the nature of the discipline, the number of hours spent in the classroom, the class format (e.g., language instruction or formal lecturing), the number of students in the class, the amount of after-class paper work performed, the time required for preparation, and whether the course is newly taught. Teaching would include one office hour per week per course for student advising. Time for thinking, which faculty do more of apparently than fee-based professionals and business executives, would be factored into the total.

To the teaching function would be added productivity units measuring *administration,* i.e., committee work, special tasks, and time spent in self-governance and peer review. The third category of the faculty workload, *research,* incorporates scholarly contributions to knowledge.

Designing productivity units for research will be difficult—which is not to state that it can't be done by a shrewd systems analyst. Comparisons must be made within disciplines. An article reporting a laboratory experiment in the natural sciences generally takes less time to produce than a scholarly article in the humanities or social sciences. But how to compare articles to books? Is a line in an article worth more or less than a line in a book? Should the quality of the journal or the publishing house be factored in? Do textbooks count? Reviews? Prizes? What about time spent on the project and results achieved?

Well, obviously, it is folly to assume any kind of precise measurement. But broad measurements are possible and useful where there is now no measurement at all. Strokes in golf, games in tennis, and minutes in a marathon declare who is the winner but they can also broadly reveal who is the professional and who is the amateur. The university's concern is not with the professionals whose productivity units are high but with the amateurs who by contrast are not achieving. Productivity units do not determine who gets the gold but who is not finishing the race—or more likely, not even entering it.

A major purpose of productivity units is to reduce labor costs while sustaining institutional eminence. As indicated earlier, a working week for a teacher is some 2 1/2 days for eight months (excluding sabbaticals). That leaves 2 1/2 days each week and four months for other activities. If the professor is not researching, he or she might reasonably be expected to teach during the other 2 1/2 days per week as well as in some kind of summer program during three of the four months.

Those who can show little evidence of research, either in notes or publications, would teach not 6 or 9 hours per week but 15 hours per week. Judicious benchmarking—identifying and emulating the institutions that are doing the best job at a task—will not turn an adoring face to Harvard! High school instructors teaching advanced students in history or literature average well over 15 hours per week in the classroom. They grade lots of tests, critique student essays, keep up in their field while at the same time they perform dreary administrative chores and resolve disciplinary emergencies during a long school year. They soldier on. Fifteen hours a week is a load that a doctor of philosophy can bear.

Periodically universities resurrect the word "constraints" like some cadaver from the cemetery of rejected proposals. The word is attached to "budget." Everyone with decision-making authority goes around muttering "due to budget constraints." Matters get serious when "budget constraints" escalates to "budget crunch." During that time of troubles metaphors call up images of slicing "fat" from the budget. As number-crunchers cry for more poundage the cuts reach to the "bone" and then finally as the bleeding campus cries for mercy the financial officer pierces to the "marrow." Other metaphors are intensified from softball to hardball (sports) to finally hand grenades (war). The departments that survive with the lowest cuts imitate the warrior's axiom: "The object of war is not to die for your country but to make the other bastard die for his."

During this ritual of carnage reporters from metropolitan dailies visit the campus and report that officials there view the cuts as nothing less than perilous to the university's acclaimed reach for excellence. Instructional cost-cutting seldom touches faculty workloads. The cuts are achieved by increasing class size, reducing the number of courses offered, and using more graduate students as teachers. Chopping a few administrators is standard. Raising tuition above the inflation rate is assured. Rarely does someone loft the option that professors teach more hours.

The possibility of increasing faculty productivity as a solution to periodic budget crises is even more discouraging when viewed from historical perspective. In the 1930s and 1940s the average teaching load for professors in the Arts & Sciences at a research university was 12 hours per week in a school year of September to June numbering 17 weeks per semester. *By the early 1990s the average load had shrunk from 12 to 6 hours per week in a school year shortened from 17 to 15 weeks per semester.*

Parents may wonder if their children seem to be home more often than memories of their own collegiate years? Wonder no more. *The school year has shortened by 12%. That's one whole month!* If the trend continues, instead of going to college with vacation breaks, students will be on vacation and take college breaks! Students will love it, since the degree carries the same value. Faculty will love it since they work fewer weeks of the year. The university will love it because they collect the same tuition whether the school year ends in June, May, or quite possibly by the end of the 1990s, in April!

Parents of children in private universities may wonder why they are paying so much for tuition. Costs obviously increase when teaching hours are cut 50% with intense pressure to hire as replacements expensive tenured faculty to expand the potential for published research. From a national viewpoint, the increased charges levied on parents would be worth it if the parents were subsidizing equivalent research that contributed to the supremacy of the United States and by extension the welfare of all humankind. That is not the case. If the university were to send home to parents a report card on productivity, it would be compelled to flunk itself.

Productivity is the measurement in both quantity and quality of the utilization of resources. Some scholars are so productive they must be on steroids. The far greater majority of professors have not contributed in research the equivalent of their cut in teaching labor. One reason the university flunks productivity is the flawed assumption that when teaching hours are reduced for everyone in a department there will be a corresponding increase by everyone in research productivity. As we suggested earlier, the differential scholarly contributions of some cannot compensate for the equal teaching loads of all.

What are the benefits of differential faculty workloads? The most obvious is a reduction in costs. And good things will happen to undergraduates. With so many professors teaching not six or nine hours but fifteen hours per week, the university will become for many students more than a dreary round of lectures, multiple-choice tests, inexperienced teaching assistants, and the apprehension of not getting a seat in a required course. To be deprived of a letter of recommendation from a mentor who can say something personal is a symbol which exposes what has become, for many of the nation's youth, an experience which is less human than it should be.

Good things will happen to those faculty who delight in teaching but have been forced to masquerade as something they are not. After tenure's comforting certitude of an annual income for life, some professors discover teaching is more satisfying than research—or they simply refuse to entomb themselves for much of that life in a laboratory or the library stacks. Let Mr. Chips be Mr. Chips! Differential faculty workloads are a face-saving alternative to the shame of a naked bibliography.

* * *

What are the chances of a serious consideration of differential faculty workloads? More than likely, alas, it's an initiative that will be viewed as DOA at the faculty committee. Powerful forces contend against differential faculty workloads.

First, givebacks are most difficult to negotiate in the academy. A university campus is not a manufacturing plant. You can't threaten to move it to Singapore. Management may coerce out of labor unions givebacks by threatening a shutdown. Shutting down a small, shaky college may be a real threat; universities are not so easily intimidated.

Second, cheaper labor is a budgetary safety valve. In universities, graduate students and adjuncts paid hourly with no fringe benefits can substitute for more expensive assistant professors. True, while the quality of the pedagogy in such courses may diminish, the numerical value of the credits earned by the students in those courses is identical.

Third, additional teaching hours cut into moonlighting. In their recent survey of higher education, Bowen and Schuster revealed that "the number of faculty who continue to teach full time while working part time at outside jobs seems to be increasing." The best deal is to teach in a "practical" discipline during the evening session at a large, non-residential city university. ("It's better at night," is the sweatshirt slogan.) The city offers the promise of jobs, even a private practice, in industries like accounting, law, finance, advertising, public relations, publishing, and in the natural sciences of health care and engineering. A faculty scattered into residential sections of the city guarantees the protection of anonymity.

The evening session is particularly desirable because it makes more workable not just a part-time job but another full-time job. There are some who work a nine-to-fiver, grab a bite to eat, and work their nine hours in the classroom three nights a week from six to nine. The other two nights are for preparation and grading papers. Weekends are generally free as are the four months of the year in which classes do not meet.

The disadvantage in the evening session used to be that the full-time workers who became part-time students in the evening were less qualified than the full-time day students. (The evening session is also where you went when you flunked out.) With the immense growth of responsible adults who worked days and studied nights, the evening session began to earn a respectability it once lacked—and a faculty who found the students challenging.

Fourth, university culture does not now consider an articulated policy of differential teaching loads an acceptable corrective to differential scholarly productivity. A protective egalitarianism within the elitism of tenured professorships forbids the adoption of differential teaching loads. In the early decades of the twentieth century, when university presidents were more powerful, teaching hours were reduced for the producers of published research. Today, one foundation reported, "it is almost impossible . . . for there to be substantial differentiation of teaching loads within a single department. As long as a few faculty members are advantaged, there will be an irresistible pressure to lower the average load."

Fifth, status quo is just fine. Bowen and Schuster in their general survey discovered that "no single finding stands out so consistently across all thirty eight campuses than the unwillingness of faculty to abandon their academic careers. They like their work, whatever its shortcomings. Indeed, many of them *love* their work. The vast majority of faculty, around 90 percent, indicated that they would choose the academic profession if they were starting over again." Who wouldn't? One professor nearing retirement echoed the point and searched for historical perspective: "When historians look back on the period 1950 to 1990 and ask what occupation was the best, they'll conclude, 'Faculty members had it best of all!'" Another explained: "Where else could I have as much freedom to do what I love to do?"

Whatever the validity of the trickle-down theory in economics, what might be called the trickle-down theory in higher education commands the certitude of gravity: Faculty workloads established for first-class research universities trickle down through doctorate-granting institutions to liberal arts colleges and community colleges. A teacher at a college that grants the masters degree expressed appropriate appreciation for the legacy: "In the lower levels of academe, like my institution, we've inherited perquisites from the higher echelon without the responsibilities of pure scholars. Thus our legacy includes twelve-hour teaching loads, the tenure system and academic freedom. Not a bad deal!"

14. CONCLUSION

Self-cleansing is not a characteristic of systems that are self-serving. So why should professors be expected to act differently than stockbrokers, realtors, architects, physicians—or generals? As we suggested at the beginning of our reconnaissance into university culture, it is not only war that is too important to be left to the generals. Most people, if given the chance, will begin to run the enterprise for themselves. If there is no competitive marketplace to keep executives faithful to the interests of shareholders, then boards of directors are responsible for protecting those shareholders from the greed of management exhibited in excessive salaries and stock options. In non-profit organizations, boards of trustees are charged with the responsibility of evaluating costs and benefits in order to protect the interests of the community and the nation.

Our queries are designed for constituents who have a stake in the university—parents, students, trustees, alumni, legislators, and taxpayers. The questions probe academic issues but are not "academic," i.e., impractical. The queries introduce specific reforms that are doable. *The reforms do not threaten the job security and income of tenured professors. They do not drain energies dedicated to increasing the prestige of the university through published research.*

The objective is to help the tenured faculty as a body do a better job at less cost—teaching undergraduates and contributing to knowledge through scholarship. It's a win-win exercise for the nation. The reforms transform a tragedy of wasted human resources, both students and professors, into a more productive educational enterprise.

The seven reforms are initiated by realistic inquiries. *Meaningful accounting*, the first, insists on interpretive numbers about how much money is actually spent on undergraduate instruction and how the faculty spends its time and with what results.

Three improve teaching. *Early retirement* enhances the quality of the instructional base by easing out incompetent teachers. *Teacher training* improves instructional effectiveness without questioning the embedded

145

academic reward system of scholarship. *Growth compacts* set up procedures for reversing faltering professorial development in both teaching and research.

Three probes reduce costs. *Peer review* for tenure appointments should be initiated by the administration in consultation with the faculty. In the traditional procedure, the faculty recommends candidates and the administration approves or vetoes. Administration origination of tenure appointments will save huge amounts of faculty time that can be spent on other pursuits while curtailing vicious political in-fighting.

Technology that replaces the professor in the classroom should be presented as a way of freeing the teacher to work interactively with students. Now there is time to analyze texts together and work through exercises in creative discovery which is the exhilaration of true learning.

Differential faculty workloads, established by productivity units, decrease costs per student. Some professors will teach many more hours than the traditional load. Others will teach fewer hours while continuing to pursue their research.

Many universities have instituted one or more of these innovations. A closer look often reveals that they but nibble at the bullet. Administrative flourishes of intent are easy to set into motion; barricades of faculty opposition mount swiftly in defense of vested interests.

* * *

Wise readers with mature experiences in the ways of institutions may have already concluded that no changes will take place because there is no whip to enforce a *perestroika*. Preeminent private universities may indeed be so paralyzed by enshrined traditions to be unable to reform themselves. Other private and public universities may be imprisoned in self-perpetuating institutional rigidities increasingly reinforced by the academic models they emulate.

If so, the last court of appeal is always national security. In the 1950s, it was Sputnik and the military threat from Soviet Russia. Today, it is the economic threat from Japan. The challenge is national performance in a global marketplace. The United States can no longer afford obsolete personnel practices in universities any more than it can tolerate sloppy workmanship in manufacturing.

APPENDIX A
THE IRONIES OF THE UNIVERSITY

The ironies listed in the Introduction are repeated in this Appendix. As noted in the Introduction, they lack the nuances which temper them in the text where they are examined more thoroughly.

- Professors are hired as teachers but evaluated as scholars.
- University presidents train to be managers by teaching and research.
- University presidents and deans enter the academic world to teach and to do research. They must stop doing what they entered the profession to do in order to to become presidents and deans. Thus promotion to acclaimed office may become a descent into professional frustration.
- University presidents and their deans do entirely different kinds of work than professors who disdain what presidents and deans do.
- University presidents diminish their authority on campus in the degree to which they build a powerful research faculty.
- University presidents create problems for themselves by enrolling minority students.
- The Dean of Students' accountability for student behavior remains consistent as the potential for irresponsible student behavior expands.
- As a university gains national recognition in football and basketball, it more than likely is staining its reputation for educational excellence.
- Universities guarantee a tenured professor an income for life while the professor may try out other colleges and return within two years if dissatisfied.
- The academic value of a credit earned by an undergraduate is the same whether taught by a full professor or a graduate student. It's also the same price.
- Universities pay for scholarly prestige, but it's owned by the professor and leaves with the departing employee.

- Universities are structured on the faith that tenured faculty will make an equal effort and contribution while in reality the effort, and particularly the contribution, are markedly unequal.

- The more expensive the tuition, the more likely a campus concern for America's "oppressed victims."

- Preferential treatment for blacks, Hispanics, and Native-Americans accentuates racial/ethnic identification in order to diminish racial/ethnic discrimination.

- Professional ethnics, hired to reduce racial/ethnic conflict, become more influential in the degree to which there is increasing racial/ethnic conflict.

- Student activists deplore the need for administrators but increase the number by requiring support staff to service their activism.

- Faculty deplore the expansion of administrators but boost their number by turning over academic advising to administrative staff.

- Federal and state governments complain about the increase in administrators while passing legislation that requires the services of administrators.

- The market value of a degree is increased, not by an improvement in the education of undergraduates, but by the faculty's enhanced reputation for scholarship.

- At least three states have passed enforcing legislation that college teachers must be proficient in English. That is, graduate students standing before a class must, as a minimum qualification, be able to speak the language of the undergraduates sitting in the class.

- At some universities, courses required for graduation are so over-enrolled that students can't complete university requirements.

- Tuition rises faster than the rate of inflation in selective private universities and colleges primarily because the demand for prestigious degrees is greater than the supply.

- An increasing endowment does not reduce tuition but inflates it.

- The progressive tuition of private universities, like a progressive income tax, soaks the qualified rich so that the qualified poor can get as good an education as the rich.

- A tuition hike is rendered more bearable for parents and students because it boosts the economic and social class value of the degree.

- As knowledge expands at an accelerating rate, a university, to remain a player, must teach and research in all the knowledge that is expanding.

- The measure of a college's performance is not the relative value added to a student from freshman to senior years but the absolute quality of the graduating senior.
- A major benefit of attending a private, high-priced university, compared to a cheaper public school, is social class identification.
- A student at a private university can pay ten times more per course taught by a graduate student than a student at a community college pays while studying under a professor with a doctorate.
- The most emphasized reason for tuition increasing above the inflation rate is labor-intensive costs. An understated reason is expensive enhancements to magnify the scholarly eminence of the university through the published research of its faculty.
- The justification for a college education is not to enjoy the life of the mind in civilized leisure but to get ahead in the world of work.
- Boards of Trustees, especially in politically sensitive public institutions, are both guardians of the university and defenders of special interest constituencies.
- Boards of Trustees and Presidents of universities get along very well together by telling one another what a great job the other is doing.
- Like art made popular by the public, a professor applauded by students raises suspicion in the faculty club of intellectual shallowness.
- Universities, specialists in education, do little to educate their educators to be effective teachers.
- University teachers hired to teach do everything they can to get out of teaching, even though a strong percentage like to teach.
- While the published research of scholars is rigorously evaluated for reliability, the undergraduate teaching of professors is seldom evaluated for the purposes of improvement.
- Professors resist technology in the degree to which the technology replaces what they do.
- Diminishing the teaching hours of non-productive professors does not result in an increase in the amount of their published research.
- For tenured professors holding two full-time jobs, teaching in the evening session is generally preferable since more jobs are available during the day.
- In the past half century the teaching hours of faculty in research institutions have been cut in half and the school year reduced by one month while teaching performance, magnified by teaching assistants, has suffered a decline in possibly equal proportions.

APPENDIX B
CARNEGIE CLASSIFICATIONS

The Carnegie Foundation for the Advancement of Teaching has classified and counted post-secondary institutions. Their categories are widely used for the statistical reporting of higher education.

The focus of this study is on the research and doctorate-granting universities. The more prestigious liberal arts colleges share in many ways similar values and faculty structure.

The Carnegie Classifications, based on the level of degree offered and comprehensiveness of mission, using figures to the year 1987, follow:

Research Universities offer a full range of baccalaureate programs, are committed to graduate education through the doctorate degree, and give a high priority to research. These institutions receive most of the research and development funding awarded by the federal government.

> (71 public and 33 private, totalling 104,
> with a student enrollment of 2,209,000.
> Student enrollment throughout this list
> includes undergraduate and graduate students
> and is based on head count)

Doctorate granting Universities are the same as research universities in offering the baccalaureate programs for undergraduates but are less committed to graduate education and receive less funding from the federal government for research.

> (63 public and 46 private, totalling 109,
> with a student enrollment of 1,220,000)

Comprehensive Universities and Colleges offer baccalaureate programs. More than half of their baccalaureate degrees are awarded in two or more occupational or professional disciplines such as engineering or business administration. Many provide graduate education through the master's degree.

> (331 public and 264 private, totalling 595,
> with a student enrollment of 3,303,000)

151

Liberal Arts Colleges are primarily undergraduate colleges.
(32 public and 540 private, totalling 572,
with a student enrollment of 584)

Two-Year Community, Junior, and Technical Colleges offer certificate or degree programs through the Associate of Arts level.
(985 public and 382 private, totalling 1,367,
with a student enrollment of 4,518,000)

Professional Schools and Other Specialized Institutions offer degrees ranging from the bachelor's to the doctorate, e.g., theological seminaries, medical centers, corporate sponsored institutions, etc.
(Total of 642
with a student enrollment of 467,000)

The total number of higher educational institutions is 3,389 with an enrollment of 12,301,000 undergraduate and graduate students.

APPENDIX C
RANKINGS

The three lists in Appendix C rank universities in the United States by specific criteria.

Association of American Universities

In Chicago in 1900 the meeting must have seemed like a Mount Olympus of educational leaders. Like Zeus, Charles William Eliot of Harvard was in the Chair. Attending court that day were Nicholas Murray Butler of Columbia, William Rainey Harper of the University of Chicago, and David Starr Jordan of Stanford University, to name a few. The number of universities at this parlay at the summit was just twelve. Could the thoughts of the university presidents gathering around Eliot have turned to an earlier Twelve? This convocation, unlike the earlier Twelve, were to spread a gospel of standards by forming an exclusive club. They called it The Association of American Universities.

A club is not a club unless you can keep somebody out. The Association now numbers only 58 institutions, of which two are Canadian. To be invited into the club a university must boast strong programs in graduate and professional education and a vigorous concentration on research. Every three years or so the Association decides if it wants to consider admitting new members. How all that takes place is as secret as Yale's Skull and Bones. The pressure for admission is intense.

Two listings are given. The alphabetical listing offers the potential for comparisons: What is the ratio of public to private? (It's approximately half and half). Of the public universities, which states are not represented? Are the universities rural or urban? What are the origins—secular or religious? If religious—Protestant, Roman Catholic, or Jewish? Of the originating group in 1900, which institutions would not be admitted today?

The chronological ordering offers a historical perspective. It reveals which institutions emerged over the decades as distinguished universities—at least by the vote of their peers, however politically petty, as we all know, that judgment can sometimes be.

Association of American Universities
(Alphabetically)

Brandeis University
Brown University
California Institute of Technology
Carnegie Mellon University
Case Western Reserve University
The Catholic University of America
Clark University
Columbia University
Cornell University
Duke University
Harvard University
Indiana University
Iowa State University
The Johns Hopkins University
Massachusettes Institute of Technology
McGill University
Michigan State University
New York University
Northwestern University
The Ohio State University
Pennsylvania State University
Princeton University
Purdue University
Rice University
Rutgers, the State University of New Jersey
Stanford University
The State University of New York at Buffalo
Syracuse University
Tulane University
University of Arizona
University of California, Berkeley
University of California, Los Angeles
University of California, San Diego
University of Chicago
University of Colorado
University of Florida
University of Illinois

University of Iowa
University of Kansas
University of Maryland
University of Michigan
University of Minnesota
University of Missouri
University of Nebraska
University of North Carolina
University of Oregon
University of Pennsylvania
University of Pittsburgh
University of Rochester
University of Southern California
University of Texas
University of Toronto
University of Virginia
University of Washington
The University of Wisconsin
Vanderbilt University
Washington University
Yale University

Association of American Universities
(In Order of Admission)

1900
The Catholic University of America
Clark University
Columbia University
Cornell University
Harvard University
The Johns Hopkins University
Princeton University
Stanford University
University of California
University of California, Berkeley
University of Chicago
University of Michigan
University of Pennsylvania
The University of Wisconsin System
Yale University

1904
University of Virginia

155

1908
University of Illinois
University of Minnesota
University of Missouri

1909
Indiana University
University of Iowa
University of Kansas
University of Nebraska

1916
The Ohio State University

1917
Northwestern University

1922
University of North Carolina

1923
Washington University

1926
McGill University
University of Toronto

1929
The University of Texas

1933
Brown University

1934
California Institute of Technology
Massachusetts Institute of Technology

1938
Duke University

1941
University of Rochester

1950
New York University
University of Washington
Vanderbilt University

1958
Iowa State University

The Pennsylvania State University
Purdue University
Tulane University

1964

Michigan State University

1966

Syracuse University
University of Colorado

1969

Case Western Reserve University
The University of Maryland
University of Oregon
University of Southern California

1974

University of California, Los Angeles
University of Pittsburgh

1982

Carnegie Mellon University
University of California, San Diego

1985

Brandeis University
Rice University
University of Arizona
University of Florida

1989

Rutgers, the State University of New Jersey
The State University of New York at Buffalo

National Science Foundation

The following list of latest figures, published by the National Science Foundation, ranks institutions by the amount received in fiscal year 1989. The heading reads: "Federal obligations for research and development to the 100 universities and colleges receiving the largest amounts."

Each institution from #1 through #22 received in federal funding for research and development in excess of $100,000,000. From #23 through #52 the amount was in excess of $50,000,000 but less than $100,000,000. From #53 through #100 the amount was in excess of $21,000,000 but less than $50,000,000.

1   The Johns Hopkins University
2   Stanford University
3   Massachusetts Institute of Technology
4   University of Washington
5   University of California, Los Angeles
6   University of Michigan
7   University of California, San Diego
8   University of California, San Francisco
9   University of Wisconsin, Madison
10 Columbia University (Main Division)
11 Yale University
12 Harvard University
13 Cornell University
14 University of Pennsylvania
15 University of California, Berkeley
16 University of Minnesota
17 Pennslyvania State University
18 University of Southern California
19 Duke University
20 Washington University
21 University of Colorado
22 University of Illinois, Urbana
23 University of Rochester
24 University of North Carolina at Chapel Hill
25 University of Pittsburgh
26 University of Chicago
27 University of Texas at Austin
28 University of Arizona
29 New York University
30 University of Iowa
31 Ohio State University

32	University of Alabama, Birmingham
33	Case Western Reserve University
34	Baylor College of Medicine
35	California Institute of Technology
36	Yeshiva University
37	Woods Hole Oceongraphic Institute
38	University of Massachusetts
39	Vanderbilt University
40	Purdue University
41	University of Utah
42	Georgia Institute of Technology
43	University of Maryland, College Park
44	University of Miami
45	University of California, Davis
46	Boston University
47	University of Florida
48	Carnegie Mellon University
49	Northwestern University
50	Indiana University
51	Michigan State University
52	University of Virginia
53	University of Texas, Southwest Medical Center—Dallas
54	University of California, Irvine
55	Princeton University
56	Tulane University
57	Emory University
58	University of Georgia
59	Texas A & M University
60	New Mexico State University
61	North Carolina State University at Raleigh
62	University of Illinois, Chicago
63	Utah State University
64	Virginia Commonwealth University
65	Oregon State University
66	State University of New York, Stony Brook
67	University of Cincinnati
68	Mt. Sinai School of Medicine
69	University of Connecticut
70	Louisiana State University
71	Tufts University
72	University of California, Santa Barbara
73	University of Hawaii, Manoa

74	Rutgers, the State University of New Jersey
75	Colorado State University
76	Rockefeller University
77	University of Maryland, Baltimore Professional School
78	Virginia Polytechnic Institute & State University
79	State University of New York, Buffalo, All Campuses
80	Brown University
81	University of Medicine and Dentistry of New Jersey
82	University of Texas Health Science Center, San Antonio
83	University of Vermont & State Agricultural College
84	University of Texas Health Science Center, Houston
85	Florida State University
86	University of Texas MD Anderson Cancer Center
87	University of Kentucky
88	Wake Forest University
89	Wayne State University
90	Iowa State University of Science and Technology
91	University of New Mexico
92	Georgetown University
93	Dartmouth College
94	University of Kansas
95	Oregon Health Sciences University
96	University of Texas Medical Branch Galveston
97	University of Missouri, Columbia
98	Temple University
99	George Washington University
100	University of Dayton

U.S. News Top 25 National Universities

The criteria used by *U.S. News & World Report* to rank national universities may be grouped into three categories—undergraduate students, faculty, and financial resources.

The undergraduate student body was measured by the acceptance rate among applicants to the 1990 entering class; the "yield" or the percentage of those accepted who actually enrolled; the enrollees' high school class standings measured by freshmen who finished in the top 10%; and either the average or midpoint combined scores on the Scholastic Aptitude Test or on the composite American College Testing Assessment.

There is a variable called "student satisfaction." It represents the average percentage of students in the 1983 to 1985 freshman classes who graduated within five years of the year they enrolled. The statistic might better have been termed the "graduation rate."

The faculty was measured by the 1990 ratio of full-time-equivalent students (FTE) to full-time-equivalent instructional faculty; the percentage of full-time faculty with doctorates or other top terminal degrees in their fields; the percentage of faculty with part-time status; and the average 1990 salary, with benefits, for tenured full professors.

The strength of a school's financial resources was determined by the 1990 dollar total of its educational and general expenditures, divided by its total full-time-equivalent enrollment.

1   Harvard University
2   Yale University
3   Stanford University
4   Princeton University
5   California Institute of Technology
6   Massachusetts Institute of Technology
7   Duke University (N.C.)
8   Dartmouth College (N.H.)
9   Columbia University (N.Y.)
10 University of Chicago
11 The Johns Hopkins University (Md.)
12 Cornell University (N.Y.)
13 University of Pennsylvania
14 Northwestern University (Ill.)
15 Rice University (Texas)
16 University of California at Berkeley
17 Brown University (R.I.)

18	Washington University (Mo.)
19	Vanderbilt University (Tenn.)
19	Georgetown University (D.C.)
21	University of Virginia
22	University of Michigan
23	University of California at Los Angeles
24	Carnegie Mellon University (Pa.)
25	University of North Carolina at Chapel Hill

U.S. News lists 179 additional national universities ranked by quartiles. The institutions are arranged alphabetically within each of the four ranked quartiles. One purpose of offering the list is to indicate the impressive number of universities competing to be players.

Quartile One

Boston College (MA)
Brandeis University (MA)
Case Western Reserve University (OH)
College of William and Mary (VA)
Emory University (GA)
Georgia Institute of Technology
Lehigh University (PA)
New York University
Penn State Univ. at University Park
Rensselaer Polytechnic Institute (NY)
Rutgers State University at New Brunswick (NJ)
SUNY at Buffalo
Tufts University (MA)
Tulane University (LA)
University of California at Davis
University of California at Irvine
University of California at San Diego
University of Florida
University of Illinois at Urbana
University of Minnesota at Twin Cities
University of Notre Dame (IN)
University of Rochester (NY)
University of Southern California
University of Texas at Austin
University of Washington
University of Wisconsin at Madison

Quartile Two

Boston University (MA)
Clark University (MA)
Clarkson University (NY)
Clemson University (SC)
Colorado School of Mines
Florida State University
Fordham University (NY)
George Washington University (DC)
Howard University (DC)
Indiana University at Bloomington
Iowa State University
Miami University (OH)
Michigan State University
North Carolina State University at Raleigh
Ohio State University
Pepperdine University (CA)
Polytechnic University (NY)
Purdue University at West Lafayette (IN)
Rutgers State University at Newark (NJ)
SUNY at Albany
SUNY at Binghamton
SUNY at Stony Brook
Southern Methodist University (TX)
Stevens Institute of Technology (NJ)
Syracuse University (NY)
Temple University (PA)
Texas A&M University at College Station
University of Alabama at Birmingham
University of Arizona
University of California at Riverside
University of California at Santa Barbara
University of Cincinnati (OH)
University of Colorado at Boulder
University of Connecticut at Storrs
University of Delaware
University of Georgia
University of Hawaii at Manoa
University of Illinois at Chicago
University of Iowa
University of Kentucky
University of Maryland at College Park

University of Miami (FL)
University of Missouri at Columbia
University of Missouri at Kansas City
University of Missouri at Rolla
University of Pittsburgh—Main Campus
University of Tennessee at Knoxville
University of Utah
University of Vermont
Virginia Tech
Yeshiva University (NY)

Quartile Three

Adelphi University (NY)
American University (DC)
Arizona State University
Auburn University—Main Campus (AL)
Baylor University (TX)
Bowling Green State University (OH)
Brigham Young University at Provo (UT)
Catholic University of America (DC)
Colorado State University
Drake University (IA)
Drexel University (PA)
Florida Atlantic University
Florida Institute of Technology
Georgia State University
Hahnemann University (PA)
Hofstra University (NY)
Illinois Institute of Technology
Kansas State University
Louisiana State University at Baton Rouge
Loyola University Chicago
Marquette University (WI)
Mississippi State University
Northeastern University (MA)
Ohio University
Oklahoma State University
Oregon State University
St. John's University (NY)
St. Louis University (MO)
Texas Christian University
University of Alabama at Tuscaloosa

University of Arkansas at Fayetteville
University of Denver (CO)
University of Houston—Main Campus (TX)
University of Idaho
University of Kansas
University of Maryland, Baltimore County
University of Massachusetts at Amherst
University of Mississippi
University of Nebraska at Lincoln
University of Nevada at Reno
University of New Hampshire
University of New Mexico—Main Campus
University of Oklahoma
University of Oregon
University of South Carolina at Columbia
University of South Florida
Utah State University
Virginia Commonwealth University
Washington State University
Wayne State University (MI)
West Virginia University

Quartile Four

Andrews University (MI)
Ball State University (IN)
Biola University (CA)
Cleveland State University (OH)
Duquesne University
East Texas State University
Idaho State University
Illinois State University
Indiana State University at Terre Haute
Kent State University
Loma Linda University at La Sierra (CA)
Louisiana Tech University
Memphis State University (TN)
Middle Tennessee State University
Mississippi College
Montana State University
New Mexico State University
New School for Social Research (NY)
North Dakota State University

Northern Arizona University
Northern Illinois University
Nova University (FL)
Old Dominion University (VA)
Portland State University (OR)
Southern Illinois University at Carbondale
Tennessee Technological University
Texas Tech University
Texas Woman's University
Union Institute (OH)
United States International University (CA)
University of Akron (OH)
University of California at Santa Cruz
University of Louisville (KY)
University of Maine at Orono
University of Missouri at St. Louis
University of Montana
University of New Orleans (LA)
University of North Carolina at Greensboro
University of North Dakota
University of North Texas
University of Northern Colorado
University of Rhode Island
University of San Francisco (CA)
University of South Dakota
University of Southern Mississippi
University of Texas at Arlington
University of Toledo (OH)
University of Tulsa (OK)
University of Wisconsin at Milwaukee
University of Wyoming
Western Michigan University

PERSONAL & ACKNOWLEDGMENTS

Personal

It's not easy criticizing higher education. It's like bad-mouthing your mother. Nourishing mother, alma mater, is how we affectionately recall where we went. It was our home-away-from-home for four years. We remember the good moments (great parties after the Big Game) and try to forget the bad times (staying up half the night cramming for an exam.) Maybe there was a teacher or two who turned us on with a passion for their subject. I had one who announced in the first class that his course was the most important we would be taking *in our entire college career.* (It was Alpheus T. Mason on political theory, and he may have been right, since events change but theory endures.)

Annie Dillard in *The Writing Life* confesses that "the life of the writer—such as it is—is colorless to the point of sensory deprivation. Many writers do little else but sit in small rooms recalling the real world. This explains why so many books describe the author's childhood. A writer's childhood may well have been the occasion of his only firsthand experience." I did escape to the "real world" of "firsthand experience" to experience personally activities central to the subject of this book. There were insights from teaching at Princeton and serving as a dean of continuing education at Hunter College of the City University of New York. The contrasts of academic culture with business culture were clarified by managing a construction-land development company and editing over thirty volumes with some thirty very individual authors.

Authors write books for a variety of reasons. Mine have taken me on journeys of reconciliation. In *The American Idea of Success* I concluded that it is possible to reconcile the conflict between the self-seeking demands of capitalism and the self-giving commands of Christianity by acknowledging that within ethical constraints a businessman can give by getting. The thoughtful reader may conclude after reading *How Professors Play the Cat Guarding the Cream* that university culture is tormented by so many ironies that reconciling the competing missions of teaching and scholarship is impossible.

The doable reforms advanced in this book try to nudge the university into confronting realistically the contending objectives. Specifically, universities must abandon the assumption of equal professorial contributions to those missions. It's an assumption cradled in the values of university culture, nourished in antiquated personnel policies, and of course jealously protected by the faculty. Corporations need plenty of reforms but are at least bludgeoned by the competition of a global marketplace; the prestigious universities examined here enjoy a secure market share and are supported by annual subsidies.

Acknowledgments

An editor's burden is revealed in the tale about a scholar who kept submitting drafts of a manuscript with a rejected paragraph. When the editor asked why he continued to include the paragraph after agreeing to reject the irrelevant material, the scholar replied: "Because it took me two weeks to research it." It is an editor's advice conversing with a scholar's consent that is the link shaping the destiny of each. Conversing with my editor, Jim Fisher, was a dialogue of amiable accord. His years as a business executive in publishing, broadened by teaching the subject, brought an unusual editorial familiarity to the subject of the book.

I heard once that Indians in the mountainous Andes always weave an imperfection into the design of their ponchos. They do it to prove that only God can create something perfect. No need to affirm divine perfection in this volume. The imperfections are my responsibility; their number has been reduced considerably by friends who have given to me a gift of their time to offer intelligent criticisms of chapters in manuscript and in some cases the entire draft. I am especially grateful to Mary A. Browne, William C. Campbell, Michael Carter, Steven Cassidy, William D.Coplin, Edward L. Davis, Jr., Charles A. Deacon, David S. Dodge, Wells Drorbaugh, Gerald Freund, Isabelle Gibb, Jeffrey L. Gilmore, Robert V. Iosue, Myron Lieberman, Ero Moussouri, David Riesman, Karen T. Roemer, Frederick Rudolph, Jaan W. Whitehead, and Stephen Wrage.

* * *

Prospero, the duke so treacherously banished in Shakespeare's *The Tempest,* was a wronged man with the right values. Cast adrift on the sea, later to land safely on a lonely island, Prospero told how he was befriended with provisions by a charitable man: "Knowing I lov'd my books, he furnish'd me from mine own library with volumes that I prize above my dukedom." My good fortune has been the availability of a largesse of libraries. The District of Columbia, with its branch libraries loaning within days to readers in other branches, boasts a trove of over one million adult titles, mostly in twentieth century Americana. Especially useful for this book were the holdings of the American Council on Education and the Office of Educational Research & Improvement Library of the United States Department of Education. The Library of Congress, of course, is a rich and dependable source, a Fort Knox of rare holdings.

There is no occupational type more nasty than a reference librarian rudely used, but none more helpful than one treated with the respect their resourcefulness deserves. They know who they are by the gratitude that I have personally expressed to them. The folks who keep the books moving across the library's circulation desk are like the cheering supporters handing cups of water to weary marathoners. Well, it's true, they can't be heard cheering very often, but their support is steady, alert, and appreciated.

February 1992   Richard M. Huber
Washington, D.C.

NOTES ON SOURCES

John Barrymore complained that having to look at a footnote was like going downstairs to answer the front door while making love. Finding an endnote in the back of a book is not only distracting but difficult to do—like playing the organ while watching a game of Ping-Pong.

The procedure here for locating sources, I hope, is reader-friendly. The sources for quotations, as well as points to be supported by citations, may be located by referring to the page numbers in the text where they appear.

INTRODUCTION

1   Michael Lewis, *Liar's Poker* (New York, 1989), p. 21. A readable point of departure on the subject of organizational culture is Terrence E. Deal and Allan A. Kennedy, *Corporate Cultures: The Rites and Rituals of Corporate Life* (Reading, MA, 1982).

CHAPTER 1. CONFLICT/CORRESPONDENCE OF INTEREST

5   The Boyer observation is from Ernest L. Boyer, *Scholarship Reconsidered: Priorities of the Professoriate* (Princeton, N.J., 1990), p. 56.

6   Adam Smith, *Wealth of Nations* (London, 1776), I, 17. The quotation, which often varies in wording when cited, is here taken from a reprint of the original 1776 edition. A comma after "baker" has been omitted for purposes of clarity.

For contemporary reflections on the nature of man from varying viewpoints, see Ian McLean, *Public Choice* (New York, 1987); Barry Schwartz, *The Battle for Human Nature* (New York, 1986); Donald L. Kanter and Philip H. Mirvis, *The Cynical Americans: Living and Working in an Age of Discontent and Disillusion* (San Francisco, 1989); Seymour Martin Lipset and William Schneider, *The Confidence Gap: Business, Labor, and Government in the Public Mind* (New York, 1983).

6   John Wesley, "The Use of Money," in *John Wesley,* ed. Albert C. Outler (New York, 1964), pp. 239–250. The phrases are repeated throughout the sermonic essay.

7   The statistics for executive compensation are from Louis Uchitelle, "No Recession for Executive Pay," *New York Times,* March 18, 1991, p. D1.

CHAPTER 2. MISSION, TRUSTEES, AND THE PRESIDENT

9   See Appendix B and Appendix C.

      The word "college" is used in this study in the generic sense of any higher educational institution.

      As explained later, the analysis of university culture does not include an athletic dimension.

9   E. Alden Dunham, *Colleges of Forgotten Americans* (New York, 1969), p. 95.

10   Howard R. Bowen and Jack H. Schuster, *American Professors* (New York, 1986), p. 150. See also, Page Smith, *Killing the Spirit: Higher Education in America* (New York, 1990), p. 198 and Martin J. Finkelstein, T*he American Academic Profession* (Columbus, Ohio, 1984), p. 120.

10   Joseph W. McGuire et al., "The Efficient Production of 'Reputation' by Prestige Research Universities in the United States," *Journal of Higher Education*, 59 (July/August 1988), 365–389, argues that the most "efficient" method of rising to a higher level of prestige is to go for a strategy of "adequate with breadth" rather than "peaks of excellence." "Breadth [in disciplines] is easier to attain than excellence, should be less expensive, and as a strategy pays off in reputation." (p. 385).

11   For a useful checklist of quantitative evaluative criteria, see Jeffrey L. Gilmore, *Price and Quality in Higher Education* (Washington, DC, 1990) (Department of Education publication). J. Wade Gilley, "U.S. News Moves Up a Rank—Barely," *AGB Reports*, 32 (November/December 1990), 35, (serial publication of the Association of Governing Boards of Universities & Colleges), challenges, as do many educators, the annual rankings of colleges and universities published in *U.S. News and World Report*. Among Gilley's criticisms is that self-reported data from universities and colleges is "questionable. . . . there is growing evidence that officials at many institutions fudge or shade their data to build up their college's or university's image."

12   The Harper quotation is from Thomas Wakefield Goodspeed, *A History of the University of Chicago Founded by John D. Rockefeller: The First Quarter-Century* (Chicago, 1916), pp. 318–319.

12   Abraham Flexner, "The Problem of College Pedagogy," *Atlantic Monthly*, 103 (June 1909), 844.

13   Frederick Rudolph, *The American College and University: A History* (New York, 1962), p. 457.

14   The point of departure for trustees, with a useful descriptive bibliography, is Clark Kerr and Marian L. Gade, *The Guardians: Boards of Trustees of American Colleges and Universities: What They Do and How Well They Do It* (Washington, DC, 1989).

15   The anecdote about the consultant is from Judith Block McLaughlin and David Riesman, *Choosing a College President* (Princeton, NJ, 1990), p. 81.

17   Stephen Joel Trachtenberg, "What's a College President? Not What He Thought It Was," *New York Times,* January 10, 1982, Section 13, p. 63. Trachtenberg is now president of George Washington University in Washington, DC.

18   For the transfer of power from president to the faculty in the transition from single-purpose teacher training colleges to multipurpose universities, see E. Alden Dunham, *Colleges of the Forgotten Americans* (New York, 1969), pp. 49–50.

19   The Hutchins quotation has been popping up for decades. An extensive search has failed to locate a printed source. Since the quotation sounds like a Hutchins crack, the attribution is to Hutchins but equivocal. I am indebted to Richard Popp at the University of Chicago archives, the historian William McNeill, and the library staff at the University of California at Santa Barbara for conducting a search.

23   At Northwestern Oklahoma State University, each year at least a few basketball players are unable to read their exams or write intelligible answers. The questions are read to them and they are graded on oral responses. Ted Gup, "Foul!" *Time,* 133 (April 3, 1989), 58.

23   Murray Sperber, *College Sports, Inc.: The Athletic Department vs. the University* (New York, 1990), p. 349. The particulars of the model offered here differ from Sperber's recommendation, but the idea is the same. For depressing reports, see Francis X. Dealy, Jr., *Win at Any Cost: The Sell Out of College Athletics* (New York, 1990) and Howard Cosell with Shelby Whitfield, *What's Wrong with Sports* (New York, 1991), pp. 38–89.

The highly publicized and earnest report of the Knight Foundation's Commission on Intercollegiate Athletics, *Keeping Faith with the Student-Athlete: A New Model for Intercollegiate Athletics* (Charlotte, NC, 1991), increases the power of university presidents over athletics. The success of the various recommended reforms depends very much on the authenticity of the independent audits of athletic affairs. Will athletic directors and booster trustees behave themselves, or will they cook the numbers? If not, increasing the authority of presidents is a blindsided trap block. Now university presidents will be blamed for a losing football team! The threatening cry will rise from the stadium: "Fire the coach and the president with the losing habit!"

An aspiring football or basketball player generally has to attend a college before joining big-time professional teams. Not so baseball. That's because professional baseball *preceded* the development of baseball in colleges. Farm clubs and a minor league became the feeders to professional baseball teams.

23   The poem is quoted in "Athletes Invoke Muse to Fight a Stereotype," *New York Times,* September 23, 1990, Section 1, p. 49.

24   The quotation is frequently cited as a *formula* for a successful college president, i.e., "sex for the students, athletics for the alumni and parking for the

faculty." Clark Kerr said they were *problems*. The comment was in response to a faculty question at an Academic Senate meeting in 1956. I am indebted to Maureen Kawaoka for digging out the precise quotation and sending it along in response to my query. Sex for the students, of course, is wittier as a *solution* than as a *problem*. However, it's not the kind of humor a chancellor would risk in the Eisenhower 1950's, hence the check on the quotation.

24   McLaughlin is quoted in "College Heads: Job's Demands," *New York Times*. April 24, 1985, p. Bl.

CHAPTER 4. THE FACULTY

30   Burton G. Malkiel, "Faculty Reflections on Teaching," in Harold T. Shapiro, *Teaching at Princeton: Report of the President, 1991* (Princeton, NJ 1991), p. 22.

32   Derek C. Bok, "350th Speech," Speech Given by President Derek C. Bok, 350th Anniversary Celebration, September 6, 1986, pp. 10–11.

32   For regulations governing faculty on outside work, see Faculty of Arts and Sciences, Harvard University, *Principles and Policies That Govern Your Research and Other Activities* (September 1989), pp. 8–9, 17; Yale University, *Faculty Handbook* (November 1986), pp. 101–103; Princeton University, *Rules and Procedures of the Faculty of Princeton University* (September 1986), pp. 78–79.

33   Harry S. Ashmore, *Unseasonable Truths: The Life of Robert Maynard Hutchins* (Boston, 1989), pp. 247–248, describes the University of Chicago requirement. I am indebted to Richard Popp at the University of Chicago Library for this reference.

33   Businessmen, of course, do serve for a fee as directors of corporations, as David Riesman correctly points out in a letter (12/21/89) to the author, but the commitment represents a different kind of service and the financial remuneration is generally modest compared to their salaries.

34   The Kendrew quotation is from Leonard Silk, "Economic Scene: New Concerns over U.S. Science," *New York Times*, March 22, 1991, p. D2.

35   Howard Cosell with Shelby Whitfield, *What's Wrong with Sports* (New York, 1991), p. 36. The usual procedure for federal funding is a peer-review system administered by individual departments and agencies. A university, bruised by rejection, may try to bypass the competitive evaluation of peers and seek an "earmarking" grant from the Congress.

37   The faculty opinion of administration is from Carnegie Foundation for the Advancement of Teaching, T*he Condition of the Professoriate: Attitudes and Trends, 1989* (Princeton, N.J.), p. 107.

CHAPTER 5. CURRICULUM—"A BUZZING CONFUSION OF COMPLAINTS"

39   *Quantity* control is much stricter, e.g., classes must be met as scheduled and final grades submitted promptly.

40   Derek Bok, "The Social Responsibilities of American Universities," Commencement Address, Harvard University, June 6, 1991, pp. 1, 7.

40   Frederick Rudolph, *Curriculum: A History of the American Undergraduate Course of Study since 1636* (San Francisco, 1977), p. 1,

41   In a "you're one, too" exchange, Thomas Spear, a teacher of African history at Williams College, accused the attacking "Right" of an ideological position "as dangerous to our democratic values today as McCarthy was in the 1950s." Thomas Spear, "Attacks on 'PC' Are New McCarthyism," *Christian Science Monitor.* April 24, 1991, p. 19.

43   The analysis of the curriculum has drawn, in addition to works cited elsewhere, on the following: Jacques Derrida, *Dissemination* (Chicago, 1981) trans. with an introduction and additional notes by Barbara Johnson; Paul de Man, *The Rhetoric of Romanticism* (New York, 1984) and *The Resistance to Theory* (Minneapolis, MI, 1986) with a foreword by Wlad Godzich; David Lehman, *Signs of the Times: Deconstruction and the Fall of Paul de Man* (New York, 1991); Rick Simonson & Scott Walker eds., *The Graywolf Annual Five: Multicultural Literacy* (Saint Paul, MI 1988); Alvin Kernan, *The Death of Literature* (New Haven, CT, 1990); George Levine et al., *Speaking for the Humanities* (New York, 1989) Occasional Paper No. 7 of the American Council of Learned Societies; Roger Kimball, *Tenured Radicals: How Politics Has Corrupted Our Higher Education* (New York, 1990); Charles J. Sykes, *The Hollow Men: Politics and Corruption in Higher Education* (Washington, DC, 1990); Elizabeth Fox-Genovese, *Feminism without Illusions: A Critique of Individualism* (Chapel Hill, NC, 1991); James Atlas, *The Book Wars* (Knoxville TN, 1990).

Among the sizeable number of magazine articles and newspaper accounts the following, in addition to those cited elsewhere, were particularly useful: Robert F. Berkhofer, Jr., "A New Context for a New American Studies?" *American Quarterly,* 41 (December 1989), 588–613; Paul Gagnon, "Multicultural and Civic Education: Can They Live Together?" *Basic Education,* 35 (May 1991), 3–5; Peter Shaw, "Making Sense of the New Academic Disciplines," *Academic Questions,* 3 (Summer 1990), 23–28; Thomas Fleming, "Revolution and Tradition in the Humanities Curriculum," *Chronicles,* 14 (September 1990), 13–16; Kenneth J. Cooper, "Coming to Grips with Diversity: At Berkeley, the Future Is Now," *Washington Post,* May 26, 1991, pp Alff.; Anthony De Palma, "Separate Ethnic Worlds Grow on Campus," *New York Times,* May 18, 1991, p. 1; Robert J. Samuelson, "The Fragmenting of America," *Washington Post,* August 7, 1991, p. A15; Laura Shapiro, "Mudslinging in Academe," *Newsweek,* 118 (July 29, 1991), 50; George F. Will, "Curdled Politics on Campus," *Newsweek,* 117 (May 6, 1991), 72 and " The Cult of Ethnicity," *Washington Post,* July 14, 1991, p. C7; Sam Howe Verhovek, "A New York Panel Urges Emphasizing Minority Cultures," *New York Times,* June 20, 1991, p. A1 and "Plan to Emphasize Minority Cultures Ignites a Debate," *New York Times,* June 21, 1991, p. A1; Tom Morganthau,

"Race on Campus: Failing the Test?" *Newsweek*, 117 (May 6, 1991), 26–27; Anne Matthews, "Deciphering Victorian Underwear and Other Seminars," *New York Times Magazine*, February 10, 1991, pp. 43 ff.; Jerry Adler, "African Dreams," *Newsweek*, 118 (September 23, 1991), 42ff.; Paul Gray, "Whose America?" *Time*, 138 (July 8, 1991), 13ff.; Harrison Rainie, "Black & White in America," *U. S. News & World Report*, 111 (July 22, 1991), 18ff.; Jerry Adler, "Taking Offense," *Newsweek*, 116 (December 24, 1990), 48ff.; Fred Siegel, "The Cult of Multiculturalism," *New Republic*, 204 (February 18, 1991), 34–40; William A. Henry III, "Upside Down in the Groves of Academe," *Time*, 137 (April 1, 1991), 66–69.

43   There are currently two organizations which have been formed to engage the issues raised in this analysis. The National Association of Scholars tilts in the direction of the cultural conservatives and is located in Princeton, New Jersey with Stephen Balch directing the operation. Teachers for a Democratic Culture tilts in the direction of the revisionists and originated in Chicago. Organized more recently, Teachers for a Democratic Culture argues that the "National Association of Scholars, their corporate foundation supporters, and like-minded writers in the press . . . are endangering education with a campaign of harassment and misrepresentation. . . . These critics make no distinction between extremists among their opposition and those who are raising legitimate questions about the relations of culture and society. . . . These critics . . . present the current debate over education . . . as a simple choice between civilization and barbarism." *Teachers for a Democratic Society* [Organizing statement, 1991], p. 1. Gerald Graff, a professor of English at the University of Chicago, has developed syllabi for undergraduate courses which engage the issues in literary texts raised by the disagreements between what we are terming the cultural conservatives and the revisionists.

For background, see Anthony DePalma, "In Campus Debate on New Orthodoxy, a Counteroffensive," *New York Times*, September 25, 1991, p. A1.

45   Matthew Arnold, *Literature and Dogma* (1873) (New York, 1883), p. 7. Whenever two or three traditionalists are gathered together, they are likely to chant the Arnoldian mantra of cultural conservatism. Arnold varied the wording. For example, several lines below the citation given here, he talked about "the best which has been thought and uttered in the world." In the Arnold quotation in the text, "in the world" follows "said." It has been omitted because "in the world" is not generally included in the citation by traditionalists.

In another essay, Arnold put it this way: "I am bound by my own definition of criticism: *a disinterested endeavor to learn and propagate the best that is known and thought in the world.*" Matthew Arnold, "The Function of Criticism at the Present Time," *Essays in Criticism* (First Series), (1865) (London, 1928), pp. 38–39. See also p. 19.

46   Professor Gertrude Himmelfarb, a persistent trumpet in the traditionalists'
      concerts of protestations, sounded a refrain for the historians: "'Politics is
      expanded to mean . . . power relations in the broadest sense—sexual,
      personal, racial, social. Thus the past itself, as well as historical writing about
      the past . . . is seen as a reflection of power relations. . . . [The proposition]
      also reduces all historical controversy to *ad hominem* arguments, since all
      historians are presumed to be expressing or defending their own positions of
      power." Gertrude Himmelfarb, "Some Reflections on the New History,"
      American Historical Review, 94 (June 1989) , 669.

46   *Writings of George Washington,* ed. John C. Fitzpatrick (Washington, 1940),
      34, p. 23.

      The "many" in *e pluribus unum* originally referred to the American colonies
      during the Revolution. It was expanded as a political metaphor to include
      the states of the Union. As a societal metaphor embracing ethnicity, it is now
      invoked in support of an assimilationist position.

47   There are at least three schools of thought within multiculturalism. One
      demands a more responsive attention to the contributions of racial and eth-
      nic groups. A second builds on that to advocate the maintenance of diversity
      with identity defined by the group. A third agrees but extends the credo to
      condemn assimilation as a conspiracy against the oppressed.

      Multicultural history is not the same as social history. Traditional social
      history examines ethnic groups, women, and social institutions without the
      value judgments of restoration, preservation, and separation.

48   Joseph Epstein, "The Joys of Victimhood," *New York Times Magazine,* July
      2, 1989, p. 40.

49   The McIntosh quotation is from William Celis 3d, "Kansas Campus
      Debates Ouster of Black Leader," *New York Times,* September 16, 1991,
      p. A14.

49   George Bush, "Remarks by the President at University of Michigan Com-
      mencement," Ann Arbor, Michigan, May 4, 1991.

      Representative statements that political correctness in the classroom was
      not widespread are Elaine El-Khawas, *Campus Trends, 1991* (Washington,
      1991), pp. 17–18, a publication of the American Council on Education; Joel
      Conarroe, "How I'm PC," *New York Times,* July 12, 1991, p. A29; and the
      report in Michael Abramowitz, "Literature Professors Look Inward and
      Find Scant Evidence of 'PC,' *Washington Post.* January 3, 1992, p. A3.

      Representative statements that PC was widespread are Edward Shils, "The
      Sad State of Humanities in America," *Wall Street Journal,* July 3, 1989, p. 5;
      Thomas Fleming, "Revolution and Tradition in the Humanities Curricu-
      lum," *Chronicles,* 14 (September 1990), 13–16; Nat Hentoff, "P.C. Thinking
      Beyond the Campus," *Responsive Community,* 1 (Summer 1991), 17–26; and
      Lynne Cheney, "Bridging Academe and American Life," *Washington Post,*
      July 15, 1991, p. All. See also the comment of the National Association of

Scholars' Stephen H. Balch questioning the validity of the American Council on Education's survey which is quoted in Kenneth J. Cooper, "'Political Correctness' Conflicts Not Widespread, College Administrators Say," *Washington Post,* July 29, 1991, p. A5.

49   In the paragraph about Thernstrom, the first and second quotations are quoted in Dinesh D'Souza, *Illiberal Education: The Politics of Race and Sex on Campus* (New York, 1991), p. 194; the third is quoted in John Taylor, "Are You Politically Correct?", *New York,* 24 (January 21, 1991), p. 34; the fourth is from Stephan Thernstrom, "McCarthyism Then and Now," *Academic Questions.* 4 (Winter 1990–91, 15.

50   The 1989 survey is Carnegie Foundation for the Advancement of Teaching, *The Condition of the Professoriate: Attitudes and Trends, 1989* (Princeton, NJ, 1989), p. 143.

50   George Orwell, *Nineteen Eighty-Four* (New York, 1949), p. 251.

51   The statistics are taken from Peter Kerr, "Cosmetic Makers Read the Census," *New York Times.* August 29, 1991, p. D1. The statistic for blacks, rounded to 13%, is 13.2%.

51   George Bush, "Excerpts from Bush's Address to General Assembly: For a 'Pax Universalis,'" *New York Times,* September 24, 1991, p. A14. The President's value judgement was made in the context of equating Zionism with racism. Marginally noted, the environment during this period was also infused with a moral dimension and lifted from a policy issue to an ethic.

52   Jawanza Kunjufu, *Lessons from History: A Celebration in Blackness –Jr.Sr. High Edition* (Chicago, Ill., 1987), p. 3.

52   The two quotations in the paragraph are from Asa G. Hilliard, "Introduction to Reprint Edition," *Stolen Legacy* by George G. M. James (1954) (San Francisco, 1988), unpaginated, and George G. M. James, *op. cit.,* pp. 7–8. A question mark at the end of the Hilliard quotation has been changed to a period without changing the meaning. Hilliard was asking if Afro-American children in schools would be interested in Herodotus' description of Egyptians. The implication is that of course they would be interested.

Other Afrocentrist writers are Molefi K. Asante, C. A. Diop, Ivan Sertima, and C. T. Cato. The Black Classic Press in Baltimore, Maryland specializes in pamphlets on Afrocentrism.

53   James Muhly, Review of *Black Athena: The Afroasiatic Roots of Classical Civilization* Volume II: *The Archaeological and Documentary Evidence* by Martin Bernal (Rutgers University Press) in *Book World* (*Washington Post*), July 21, 1991, pp. 3 ff.

The style of Afrocentrist writing unfortunately does not permit us to retreat behind the Italian maxim: *Se non e vero, e ben trovato* or, it need not be true as long as it is well said.

For Afrocentrism and the public schools, see Michel Marriott, "Afrocentrism: Balancing or Skewing History?", *New York Times,* August 11, 1991, Section 1, pp. 1ff.

53   Samuel Francis, "Principalities & Powers," *Chronicles,* 15 (February 1991), 9; Diane Ravitch, "History and the Perils of Pride," *Perspectives,* 29 (March 1991), 13.

       See, also, Diane Ravitch, "Pluralism vs. particularism in American Education," *Responsive Community,* 1 (Spring 1991), 32–45. Ravitch makes a distinction between "pluralistic multiculturalism" which stresses a more unifying responsibility for each other and "particularistic multiculturalism." The particularists "neglect the bonds of mutuality that exist among people of different groups and encourage children to seek their primary identity in the cultures and homelands of their ancestors." (p. 33). The multiculturalism referred to in this chapter is particularistic rather than pluralistic. Ravitch was appointed to the policymaking position of Assistant Secretary for the Office of Educational Research and Improvement in the United States Department of Education in 1991.

53   The high school student is quoted in Peter Applebome, "Valedictorian Issue a Mirror of Race Tension at a School," *New York Times,* June 8, 1991, pp. 1ff. On the graduate school level, see Richard Blow, "Mea Culpa," *New Republic,* 204 (February 18, 1991), 32.

54   Milot is quoted in Dinesh D'Souza, *Illiberal Education: The Politics of Race and Sex on Campus* (New York, 1991), p. 131; Arthur M. Schlesinger, Jr., *The Disuniting of America* (Knoxville, TN, 1991), p. 77. See also Mark Whitaker, "A Crisis of Shattered Dreams," *Newsweek,* 117 (May 6, 1991), 28.

54   The Sobel quotation is from Joseph Berger, "Education Chief: At Eye of Diversity Storm," *New York Times,* August 1, 1991, pp. Blff. Italics have been added.

55   Center for the Teaching and Study of American Cultures, *American Cultures at the University of California at Berkeley* (Berkeley, CA, 1991). See also Kenneth J. Cooper, "'American Cultures' at Berkeley: Requiring a Variety of Perspectives," *Washington Post,* May 27, 1991, p. Al.

CHAPTER 6. CURRICULUM—MULTICULTURALISM

57   The punctuation and wording for the chant, which varies, is taken from the January 16, 1987 press release of the Stanford University News Service reporting the vote of the faculty senate on western culture courses. See also the memorandum of Bob Beyers of April 17, 1991 released by the Stanford University News Service attempting to correct press inaccuracies. Several well-publicized incidents about multiculturalism, such as the Jesse Jackson appearance at Stanford, have been invoked for illustrative purposes because they are now cemented into the evidence. Unfortunately, the reports at the time, and then repeated in the press, were not always accurate, which explains the need for the correctives.

57   Henry Louis Gates, Jr. "Whose Culture Is It, Anyway?: It's Not Just Anglo-Saxon," *New York Times*, May 4, 1991, p. 23. Gates Op-Ed piece was published after he was appointed to Harvard but before assuming the position. See, also, the African-American view in the OP-Ed piece of Hugh B. Price, "The Mosaic and the Melting Pot," *New York Times*, September 23, 1991, p. A17. Price is vice president of the Rockefeller Foundation.

58   Donald Kagan, "Whose Culture Is It, Anyway?: Western Values Are Central," *New York Times*, May 4, 1991, p. 23. An Op-Ed piece.

58   Dinesh D'Souza, "The Politics of Force-Fed Multiculturalism," *Christian Science Monitor*, April 22, 1991, p. 19.

58   Forrest McDonald, "On the Study of History," *Chronicles*, 15 (February 1991), 16. A more gentle approach is taken by Jacob Neusner, "It Is Time to Stop Apologizing for Western Civilization and to Start Analyzing Why It Defines World Culture," *Chronicle of Higher Education*, February 15, 1989, pp. Bl–B2.

    The novelist Saul Bellow is sometimes, without a citation, quoted with the query: "Who is the Tolstoy of the Zulus? The Proust of the Papuans? I'd be glad to read him." The crack sounds like a putdown, but Bellow has said that he meant something quite different, whatever the exact wording originally expressed in a telephone conversation with an unremembered person. He meant that pre-literate societies, without a written language, obviously have no literary equivalent of Tolstoy or Proust. (Letter from Saul Bellow to the author, dated October 8, 1991.)

60   Honing is quoted in Robert Reinhold, "Class Struggle," *New York Times Magazine*, September 29, 1991, pp. 27, 47.

60   E. D. Hirsch, Jr., *Cultural Literacy: What Every American Needs to Know* (Boston, 1987), p. 93.

61   The Long quotation is from Malcolm Jones, Jr. "It's a Not So Small World," *Newsweek*, 118 (September 9, 1991), 64. The Canavan quotation is from Lisa Leff, "Pr. George's Curriculum Expands the Culture of the Classroom," *Washington Post*, September 9, 1991, pp. Dl ff.

62   The Jordan quotation is from Ira Berkow, "Jordan Tries, So Don't Be 'Stoopid,'" *New York Times*. September 2, 1991, p. 37.

62   The report about the University of Pennsylvania is from Alan Charles Kors, "The Politicization of the University, In Loco Parentis," *The World & I*, 6 (May 1991), 492–493. Kors, a history professor at the University of Pennsylvania, cited the undergraduate's memo in his article "It's Speech, Not Sex, the Dean Bans Now," *Wall Street Journal*, October 12, 1989, p. A16. The University responded to the widely reported implication of censorship, pointing out that the administrator was not coercing the student. President Sheldon Hackney explained, rather, that the correspondence was "a great example of a free and open exchange of ideas among members of the university community on a very complex and timely issue. . . ." (Sheldon Hackney,

"In the PC Wars: A Message from the Front," p. 2—an undated address supplied by the Office of University Relations in a letter dated September 6, 1991.)

In fairness, the report is taken from a later account in *The World & I* where there is no implication of censorship. Kors, however, could not resist calling the memorandum writer a "courageous female undergraduate." (p. 491)

62 The sequence of the citations from Steele in the three paragraphs are Shelby Steele, *The Content of Our Character: A New Vision of Race in America* (New York, 1990), pp. 130, 132, 140, 141, 148. For an Hispanic view, see Linda Chavez, *Out of the Barrio: Toward a New Politics of Hispanic Assimilation* (New York, 1991).

63 Stephen L. Carter, *Reflections of an Affirmative Action Baby,* (New York, 1991), pp. 49, 52.

64 Woodrow Wilson, "An Address in Philadelphia to Newly Naturalized Citizens," May 10, 1915 in *The Papers of Woodrow Wilson,* eds. Arthur S. Link, David W. Hirst et al., (Princeton, NJ, 1980), vol. 33, p. 148.

65 The Schlesinger quotation is from Arthur M. Schlesinger, Jr., *The Disuniting of America* (Knoxville, TN, 1991), p. 20. There's a Shaw concordance of the plays, but the quotation was not listed. The quip sounds Shavian and may appear in a letter.

Anthony DePalma, "Higher Education Feels the Heat," *New York Times,* June 2, 1991, Section 4, pp. 1ff., reported that "the splendid seclusion of the university has been shattered by a barrage of criticism. . . ." From multiculturalism to federal funding, higher education was moving onto the front page of the nation's press.

65 The Busnardo quotation is from Dirk Johnson, "Denver Journal: As Discoverer is Hailed, the Discovered Protest," *New York Times,* October 14, 1991, p. A8. As noted earlier, a multicultural approach is not the same as social history.

66 Commission on Higher Education of the Middle States Association of Colleges and Schools, *Characteristics of Excellence in Higher Education: Standards for Accreditation* (Philadelphia, 1990), pp. 14, 16.

67 The methodological problems of measuring the economic, artistic, intellectual, etc. contributions of various ethnic groups to American society contain so many variables that it is sensible to avoid the issue. Food, however, is easy, since the obvious winners are French and Chinese . . . whoa . . . how about Vietnamese, Indian, northern Italian . . . There is probably general agreement on the loser list, leading off with the British.

67 The Japanese quotation and the account are from Steven R. Weisman, "Japanese Coin a Word for New Feeling about U.S.," *New York Times,* October 16, 1991, p. A14.

67 Alexis de Tocqueville, *Selected Letters on Politics and Society,* ed. Roger Boesche (Berkeley and Los Angeles, 1985), p. 38.

68   The Hickman quotation is from Peter Applebome, "Despite Talk of Sexual Harassment, Thomas Hearings Turned on Race Issue," *New York Times*, October 19, 1991, p. 8. Bradlee is quoted in Ken Adelman, "So Long, Sweetheart," *Washingtonian*, 26 (September 1991), 126. Frankie's search is from Carson McCullers, *The Member of the Wedding* (New York, 1951), p. 52. The play was produced in New York in 1950; the novel was published in 1946.

For a history of the ideology of cultural pluralism, see the essays in *Harvard Encyclopedia of American Ethnic Groups* (Cambridge, Mass., 1980) by Philip Gleason, Harold J. Abramson, and William Petersen. Also, see John Higham, *Send These to Me* (New York, 1975), pp. 196–246. Higham offers an interesting historical observation: "Integration in its modern form expresses the universalism of the Enlightenment. Pluralism rests on the diversitarian premises of romantic thought." (p. 232)

69   A taboo subject about race is a genetic determination of group differences, e.g., assessing mental abilities or measuring athletic prowess. Group differences are to be explained by environmental conditioning. As a practical matter, cosmetic surgeons do consider genetic differences in bone structure and skin quality when operating on caucasians, blacks, and asians. See Elisabeth Rosenthal, "Ethnic Ideals: Rethinking Plastic Surgery," *New York Times*, September 25, 1991, p. Cl.

70   In the Italian-American paragraph, the first quotation is from Joseph V. Scelsa, *Italian-American Affairs at the City University of New York: Historical Overview* (New York, no date), p. 4. The remaining quotations are from Complaint of Italian-American Legal Defense and Higher Education Fund, Inc., "A Brief History of Discrimination Against Italian-Americans at the City University of New York," (filed July 27, 1990) , pp. 1, 2, 3.

The directive designating Italian-Americans as an affirmative action category is confirmed in the memorandum of Chancellor Robert J. Kibbee to CUNY Council of Presidents, December 9, 1976.

70   The quotation of the Williams college student is from Alison Gendar, "Minority Students Seek Reform," *Berkshire Eagle*, April 23, 1988, pp. 1ff., and is cited in Dinesh D'Souza, *Illiberal Education: The Politics of Race and Sex on Campus* (New York, 1991), p. 170. The word "are" in the D'Souza recording has been changed to "is" to correspond with the precise quotation in the newspaper document. The Wilson position is reported in Carolyn J. Mooney, "Affirmative-Action Goals, Coupled with Tiny Number of Minority Ph.D's, Set Off Faculty Recruiting Frenzy," *Chronicle of Higher Education*, August 2, 1989, pp. 1ff.

70   William Safire, "On Language: Hyphenated Americans," *New York Times Magazine*, July 28, 1991, p. 10. The italicizing of the hyphenated designations has been omitted.

71   The quotation on stereotyping is from "Style Plus," *Washington Post*, July 2, 1991, p. E5.

72 For ethnic jokes, see, for example, Blanche Knott, *Truly Tasteless Jokes Two* (New York, 1983); Maude Thickett, *Outrageously Offensive Jokes* (New York, 1983); Julius Alvin, *Totally Gross Jokes* (New York, 1983). Irving Lewis Allen, *Unkind Words: Ethnic Labeling from Redskin to WASP* (New York, 1990), is a recent work of readable scholarship from a lexical perspective.

72 The Denver report and Beck observation are from Dirk Johnson, "With This Tough Audience, Fair-Haired is Fair Game," *New York Times*, November 3, 1991, Section 4, p. 5.

75 For statistics on legacies, see John Larew, "Why Are Droves of Unqualified, Unprepared Kids Getting into Our Top Colleges?," *Washington Monthly*, 23 (June 1991), 10–14.

CHAPTER 7. STUDENTS

79 The Harvard and Stanford anecdotes are from Jacques Steinberg, "Admissions Ploys That Backfire," *New York Times*, November 11, 1990, Section 4A, p. 10.

80 The Directors of Admissions anecdotes are from Richard Moll, *Playing the Private College Admissions Game* (New York, 1986), pp. 213–214.

82 The student is quoted in Robin Wilson, "Undergraduates at Large Universities Found to Be Increasingly Dissatisfied," *Chronicle of Higher Education*, January 9, 1991, p. A38. The friend of Stanford is quoted in Donald Kennedy, "Stanford in Its Second Century," An Address to the Stanford Community by President Donald Kennedy, April 5, 1990, p. 11.

83 The complaints about undergraduate education are from Robin Wilson, *op. cit.*, p. A38.

84 Report of the Commission on Responses to a Changing Student Body, *Promoting Student Success at Berkeley: Guidelines for the Future* (Berkeley, CA, 1991), p. 15.

84 On teaching assistants, see reports in the *New York Times*, July 11, 1990, p. B9; November 5, 1990, p. 12; November 11, 1990, pp. A1 ff.

84 The Toledo dean is quoted in Karen De Witt, "Student Protest Movement Expands, and Its Voice Is That of the Consumer," *New York Times*, October 17, 1990, p. B6. See also reports in *New York Times*, December 23, 1990, Section 1, p. 30, and February 11, 1991, p. A1.

85 The Coplin quotation in the first paragraph is from William D. Coplin, "Undergraduates for a Better Education—A Lesson in Politics," *Political Science Teacher*, 3 (Fall 1990), 18, and in the second paragraph from p. 19. Coplin parenthetically notes in the quotation that "I am still having trouble convincing them and myself that there are no Dengs among the faculty."

David N. Smith, *Who Rules the Universities? An Essay in Class Analysis* (New York, 1974), is a contrasting Marxist interpretation which sees students as "apprentice workers" (p. 15) and advocates the development of "the revolutionary class consciousness necessary for the elimination of class exploitation and the creation of socialism." Smith offers a theory for students and college-educated workers that "makes sense of their experience in society and enables them to understand the class nature of their oppression and struggle." (p. 14)

For a shopping list of politicized "demands" more reminiscent of the 1960s than a student consumer movement, see Herbert London, "From the Editor's Desk: The Rites of Spring at Hunter College," *Academic Questions* , 4 (Winter 1990–91), 9–10.

86   The Levine anecdote is from John A. Byrne, "The Best B-Schools," *Business Week,* Number 3185 (October 29, 1990), 58.

87   Hastings Rashdall, *The Universities of Europe in the Middle Ages* (1895) (London, 1936). The quotation in the first paragraph about Bologna is from p. 196, in the second from p. 197. A colon after "rectors" has been changed to a period for purposes of clarity.

CHAPTER 8. TUITION—STICKER PRICE

89   Fred Hargadon, "Chances for Admission, Then and Now," *Princeton Alumni Weekly*, 90 (December 20, 1989), first verso.

At Georgetown University, to cite another illustration, for the Class of 1989 there were 10,662 candidates for 1,301 places. Acceptances were sent to 2,517 candidates. Georgetown accepted for admission 24% and of that number 52% chose to enroll. The Dean of Admissions, Charles A. Deacon, estimates that "well over 9,000 would have been well qualified to handle the academic work at Georgetown." Letter to author, July 20, 1990.

On selectivity, *Barron's Profiles of American Colleges* (New York, 1991), pp. 250–252, reports that there are 92 colleges and universities which accept fewer than one third of their applicants and 163 which accept fewer than one half. Terry W. Hartle in Barry Werth, "Why Is College So Expensive," *Change,* 20 (March/April 1988), 23 states that "there may be 75 schools . . . where demand is relatively insensitive to the price charged." Chester E. Finn, Jr., "Education Reform vs. Civil Rights Agendas," *New York Times*, May 18, 1991, p. 23, (an Op-Ed piece), estimates that some 50 colleges reject more applicants than they admit.

89   Williams is quoted in "Lessons," *New York Times*, March 23, 1988, p. B9.

90   Businesses and universities are *not* alike when the service costs more for one customer than another. Businesses usually charge more; universities charge pretty much the same for a Chemistry degree, with expensive laboratory equipment, as they do for a degree in philosophy.

92   The quotation is from the May 22, 1991 Justice Department press release from the Professions and Intellectual Property Section, Antitrust Division, U.S. Department of Justice titled "Consent Decree Settles Charge of Conspiracy to Restrain Price Competition on Financial Aid Against Major Universities." For background, see Anthony DePalma, "Colleges Block An-

titrust Charge by Ending Collaboration on Aid," *New York Times* , May 23, 1991, p. A1, and Sharon LaFraniere, "Ivy League Schools Agree to Halt Collaboration on Financial Aid," *Washington Post*, May 23, 1991, p. A3.

93   Freedman is quoted in "Bok to Step Aside at Harvard, Ending 20 Years as President," *New York Times*, May 30, 1990, pp 1ff. Italics have been added.

CHAPTER 9. TUITION—COSTS AND BENEFITS

98   The comparative statistics on earning power were provided by Thomas D. Snyder, National Center for Education Statistics, Department of Education, in an interview on January 21, 1992.

98   The statistics on enrollment in graduate or professional schools is from an interview with Thomas D. Snyder, National Center for Education Statistics, Department of Education, January 21, 1992.

98   Lynne V. Cheney, *Tyrannical Machines* (Washington, DC, 1990, p. 39. Guidebooks with intriguing selective criteria are Richard Moll, *The Public Ivys: A Guide to America's Best Public Undergraduate Colleges and Universities* (New York, 1985), and Martin Nemko, *How to Get an Ivy League Education at a State University* (New York, 1988).

Guidebooks vary in their attention to the quality of undergraduate teaching. Some measurements used are the percentage of Ph.Ds on the faculty, emphasis on teaching vs. research in promotions, percentage of classes taught by teaching assistants, existence of teacher training programs for TA's, class size, student evaluations of teaching, and availability of faculty.

Senior Writer John A. Byrne took *Business Week* into a pioneering venture in higher education. He surveyed graduates of Business Schools which offered the Masters Degree and the recruiters who visited the schools. The result was a consumer satisfaction index provided by the graduates and an employer evaluation index submitted by the recruiters. He then ranked the B-schools, much to the distress of some—and the immodest jubilation of others. John A. Byrne, "The Best B-Schools," *Business Week,* number 3081 (November 28, 1988), 76ff. and number 3185 (October 29, 1990), 52ff. See, also, John A. Byrne, "Back to School: The B-Schools That Are Best in Executive Education," *Business Week,* number 3237 (October 29, 1991), 102ff. For another ranking of business schools, and in addition schools of law, medicine, and engineering, see Robert J. Morse, "The Best Graduate Schools ," *U.S. News & World Report,* 110 (April 29, 1991), 62ff.

99   The ratio of three to one is obviously not exact for every comparison. Whether the ratio is two to one or four or six to one does not alter the interpretive point of contrasting higher educational institutions from this angle of vision.

101   The translation of economic class into social class is examined in Richard M. Huber, *The American Idea of Success* (1971) (Wainscott, NY, 1987).

101 John Grier Hibben was president of Princeton University from 1912 to 1932. Despite a search of relevant material, the quotation remains oral and anecdotal.

CHAPTER 10. TUITION—WHERE IT GOES

103 The tuition increases during the 1980s are bracketed by 1979–1980 and 1989–1990 and are calculated from National Center for Education Statistics, *Digest of Education Statistics: 1991* (Washington, 1991), pp. 40, 296, 297.

Over the past half-century college charges rose a percentage point or two per year above the inflation rate until the latter part of the 1970s when tuition grew more slowly than inflation. The sharp acceleration rate of the 1980s, therefore, is an aberration. See Arthur M. Hauptman with Jamie P. Merisotis, *The College Spiral* (New York, 1990), p. 1. Student fees are sometimes separate from tuition. They are combined in this study.

For additional analyses of tuition increases, see Michael O'Keefe, "College Costs," *Change*, 18 (May/June 1986), 6–8; Barry Werth, "Why Is College So Expensive?" *Change*, 20 (March/April 1988), 13–25; Bruce M. Carnes, "The Campus Cost Explosion," *Policy Review*, 40 (Spring 1987), 68–71.

103 The beliefs about the value of a college education are from Gallup Organization, *Attitudes about American Colleges 1991* (Princeton, NJ, 1991), p. 3. The survey was commissioned by the Council for the Advancement and Support of Education (CASE). A revealing finding for ethnic values was that a striking 86% of blacks said a college degree was very important while the figure for "Hispanic (not black)" was 62%. The figure for "white (non-Hispanic)" was 72%. (p. 4)

105 John Wesley, "The Use of Money," in John Wesley, ed. Albert C. Outler (New York, 1964), pp. 239–250. The phrases are repeated throughout the essay.

106 The statistics on fewer students and more professors is from William G. Bowen and Julie Ann Sosa, *Prospects for Faculty in the Arts and Sciences* (Princeton, NJ, 1989), pp. 71–72. The dates are 1976–77 to 1986–87. The precise percentages are 14.2 and 16.3. There is no evidence that the sharp drop in the student/faculty ratio resulted in smaller classes, particularly in research universities. The arts-and- science faculty does, of course, teach courses attended by students studying for non-arts-and-sciences degrees, e.g., engineering, business, etc.

106 Carol Frances, *What Factors Affect College Tuition?* (Washington, 1990), points out that "the reason the rate of increase in tuition did not come down as fast as the CPI [Consumer Price Index] is, partly, that students are paying a larger *share* of the costs of their education." (p. v)

107 For a discussion linking tuition to per-student-costs in the nation's largest comprehensive public university system, State University of New York, see Board of Trustees Ad Hoc Committee on University Revenue and Tuition

Policy, *Report to the Board of Trustees on University Revenue and Tuition Policy*, (Albany, NY, 1991).

108   In calculating the percentage that students pay through tuition for their instructional costs, it is important to be precise about what the statistic refers to: Extent of costs (total or instructional) and type of institution (two or four year, public or private, research or teaching oriented.) Even when the variables are specified, the numbers vary widely. Whatever the imprecise national figures, an interested citizen does not have to be a certified public accountant to allocate costs for a specific institution.

Lynne V. Cheney, *Tyrannical Machines* (Washington, 1990), p. 28, states that instructional budgets typically comprise "40 percent of educational and general expenditures" for four-year institutions. A faculty committee at the Massachusetts Institute of Technology in 1991 stated that "undergraduate tuition covers only about one-third of the total cost of education, the remainder being made up from endowment income, fees, and other sources, including some Federal support." Faculty Study Group, *The International Relationships of MIT in a Technologically Competitive World* (May 1, 1991), p. 13. Kent Halstead, *Higher Education Tuition* (Washington, 1989), concluded at the end of the 1980s that "in the public sector, students pay only about one-fifth the total cost, in the private sector about four-fifths." (p. 1)

It costs approximately three times more to educate a graduate student than an undergraduate. Duc-Le To, *Estimating the Cost of a Bachelor's Degree: An Institutional Analysis* (Washington, 1987), p. 14.

109   College Entrance Examination Board, *Meeting College Costs* (New York, 1990) is a brief, clear statement on applying for financial aid. Grants are usually based on need; scholarships on need and other criteria such as academic achievement.

The percentage of undergraduates receiving *federal* financial aid in the fall of 1986, the latest figures, was 34.9% and receiving *non-federal* aid was 28.8%. The percentage of undergraduates receiving any aid was 45.5%. National Center for Education Statistics, *Digest of Education Statistics: 1990* (Washington, 1991), Table 282, p. 287.

CHAPTER 11. EVALUATION & SOME FOLLIES

111   Clark Kerr and Marian L. Gade, *The Guardians: Boards of Trustees of American Colleges and Universities* (Washington, D.C., 1989), p. 7.

The quantity of higher education is also impressive. Higher education accounts for 40% of all money spent on non-corporate education in the United States amounting to 155 billion dollars representing almost 3% of the gross national product. Statistics from Thomas D. Snyder, National Center for Education Statistics, Department of Education, January 14, 1992.

112   Seventy-five percent of all dollars spent on campus for research is federally supported. This statistic, and the one about basic research, is from Arthur

M. Hauptman with Jamie P. Merisotis, *The College Tuition Spiral* (New York, 1990), p. 84. The cross cultural comparison about the percentage of the American population attending college is confirmed in a telephone conversation with Thomas D. Snyder, National Center for Education Statistics, U. S. Department of Education, January 6, 1992.

A lot is known about how wealth increases but very little about how knowledge increases. For a rare negative view of the university's role in the contribution to knowledge, see W. W. Bartley III, *Unfathomed Knowledge, Unmeasured Wealth: On Universities and the Wealth of Nations* (La Salle, IL, 1990).

112 The faculty satisfaction poll is from Alexander W. Astin et al., *The American College Teacher: National Norms for the 1989–90 HERI Faculty Survey* (Los Angeles, 1991), p. 20, Table 10.

For the Graduate Record Exam (GRE) and professional school admission tests, see Robert J. Samuelson, "School Reform Fraud (Cont'd)," *Newsweek*, 118 (October 28, 1991), 51, and National Center for Education Statistics, *Digest of Education Statistics: 1991* (Washington, 1991), p. 295. The evidence is weak because the test- takers and the tests may not have been consistent. Marginally noted, in the GRE subject tests, test results rose in the natural sciences with mathematics leading and fell in the social sciences and humanities with political science and sociology at the bottom.

Daniel J. Singal, "The Other Crisis in American Education," *Atlantic Monthly*, 268 (November 1991), 59–74, is an important article decrying the intellectual competence of even the brighter undergraduates, reaching beyond the attention to inner city schools to the serious failure of suburban high schools since the permissive 1960s.

113 Ernest L. Boyer, *Scholarship Reconsidered: Priorities of the Professoriate* (Princeton, NJ, 1990), p. 55. The quotation within the Boyer citation is from Ernest A. Lynton and Sandra E. Elman, *New Priorities for the University* (San Francisco, 1987), p. 13.

114 David E. Rosenbaum, "The Canon Has Changed, the Keg Is Ever the Same," *New York Times*, June 2, 1991, Section 4, p. 5.

114 Scott Donaldson, *John Cheever: A Biography* (New York, 1988), p. x. Regrettably, the source of the widow's comment cannot be recalled, but it probably is from a short story or novel.

114 Thomas Colley Grattan, *Civilized America* (London, 1859), II, 320.

116 For modern literature and the arts, cf. Eugen Weber, Western Tradition television series funded by Annenberg/CPB.

117 Two approaches to vouchers, or similar plans, for public schools are Myron Lieberman, *Privatization and Educational Choice* (New York, 1989) and John E. Chubb and Terry M. Moe, *Politics, Markets, and America's Schools* (Washington, 1990).

118 "All the Teachers Must Be Good," *Journal Star*, [Peoria, Illinois], June 25, 1991, an editorial. The charges against Harker are listed in the transcript of the hearing dated October 18, 1990, pp. 3–4.

118 Cicero, Pro Cluentio 53. "Unquestionably the tenure system has dangers," concluded one academic administrator, "but none is as great as those that would attend its abandonment." Steven M. Cahn, *Saints and Scamps: Ethics in Academia* (Totowa, NJ, 1986), p. 76.

119 The Gould quotation is from "Balancing Teaching and Writing," *Journal of the Harvard-Danforth Center on Teaching and Learning*, 2 (January 1987), 16.

CHAPTER 12. DOABLES—IMPROVE QUALITY

121 The quotation is from a telephone conversation with Peter Drucker on June 10, 1991.

121 The quotation from a professor at a top research university is from Ernest L. Boyer, *Scholarship Reconsidered: Priorities of the Professoriate* (Princeton, NJ, 1990), p. 33.

122 Bill McAllister, "Stanford Chief Quits over Billings Flap," *Washington Post*, July 30, 1991, p. A1, lists the charges against Stanford.

122 The Dingell quotation is from Richard L. Berke, "Dingell vs. Academia," *New York Times*, April 4, 1991, Section 4, p. 4. For background, see Karen de Witt, "Stanford, Criticized on Research Costs, Alters Billing System," *New York Times*, March 14, 1991, p. A23, and Susan Tifft, "Scandal in the Laboratories," *Time*, 137 (March 18, 1991), 74–75.

The Office of Management and Budget establishes the principles for applicable costs in *Circular No. A-21* (with revisions.) The overhead rate for each university is negotiated with one of three U.S. agencies: the Departments of Defense, Energy, or Health and Human Services.

In an ongoing audit, the Inspector General for the Department of Health and Human Services weighed in with the damaging results of an investigation into 14 colleges and universities. (Common Identification Number A-01-9 1-04008, dated December 1991). The danger in an audit frenzy, of course, is that the auditors begin to reinterpret "unallowable costs." What seemed to be approved is now judged to be not permissible. Still, Christmas cards at $2,425? (p. 11)

An example of the operational differences between public and private universities is the persistence with which private universities look for allowable expenses. At the end of the fiscal year, private universities carry over balances into the next fiscal year. State universities generally have to hand over the money to the state government. The incentive in state schools is not to save but to spend. Also, state taxes are there to help cover heat, light, and other overhead expenses connected with research.

123 The Massy and Biddle quotations are from Kenneth J. Cooper, "Universities' Images Stained by Improper Charges to Government," *Washington*

Post, May 6, 1991. p. A13. Paul Biddle was awarded a Navy Meritorious Civilian Service Award for his role in revealing how Stanford overcharged the government. Kenneth J. Cooper, "Navy to Honor Biddle's Campus Crusade," *Washington Post*, September 30, 1991, p. A9.

123   The Bennett quotation is from R. L. Berke, *op. cit.*, p. 4.

125   The quotation about the absence of rewards for teaching is from Carnegie Foundation for the Advancement of Teaching, *Campus Life: In Search of Community* (Princeton, N.J., 1990), p.12.

126   The quotations from college administrators are from Francis C. Rosecrance, *The American College and Its Teachers* (New York, 1962), p. 209.

126   Edmund Ezra Day, "Competition between Teaching and Research in American Universities," in *Education for Freedom and Responsibility: Selected Essays by Edmund Ezra Day*, ed. Milton R. Konvitz (Ithaca, NY 1952), p. 100. The speech was originally published in 1940.

127   The Chekhov confession is in a letter to J. I. Ostrovsky, dated February 11, 1893. Avrahm Yarmolinsky, *Letters of Anton Chekhov* (New York, 1973), p. 230. See p. 44 for a variation on the theme.

127   Martin J. Finkelstein, *The American Academic Profession* (Columbus, Ohio, 1984), p. 126. Harold E. Yuker, *Faculty Workload: Research, Theory, and Interpretation* (Washington, 1984), p. 47. See, also, Hugh S. Brown and Lewis B. Mayhew, *American Higher Education* (New York, 1965), p. 69.

128   The quotation about the evaluative opinions of faculty and students on teaching is from M. J. Finkelstein, *op.cit.*, p. 126.

128   Chester E. Finn, Jr., "Trying Higher Education: An Eight Count Indictment," *Change*, 16 (May/June 1984), 48.

128   The quotation and the statistics about teaching assistants is from Peter Monaghan, "University Officials Deplore the Lack of Adequate Training Given to Teaching Assistants, Ponder How to Improve It," *Chronicle of Higher Education*, November 29, 1989, p. A17. For background, see Don Wycliff, "Concern Grows on Campuses at Teaching's Loss of Status," *New York Times*, September 4, 1990, pp. A 1ff.

128   Edmund Ezra Day, *op. cit.*, pp. 104–105.

An Association of American Universities' memorandum (untitled), dated September 10, 1990, indicates that the nation's most prestigious universities are beginning to take some action to improve undergraduate teaching. The lofty rhetoric, however, must be measured against how systematic, required, and extensive the programs are for teaching assistants and tenured faculty, and by the enforcement of evaluative follow-up procedures.

130   Ernest L. Boyer, *Scholarship Reconsidered: Priorities of the Professoriate* (Princeton, N.J., 1990), p. 44, gives the statistics on the interest in teaching.

131   A point of departure for faculty development is Sherry L. Willis and Samuel S. Dubin eds., *Maintaining Professional Competence: Approaches to Career*

Enhancement, Vitality, and Success through a Work Life (San Francisco, 1990), a series of essays with recent references.

132 Hand-holding guides to assist institutions serious about the improvement of teaching are available. A sampling is: Robert B. Kozma et al., *Instructional Techniques in Higher Education* (Englewood Cliffs, N J, 1978); Joseph Katz and Mildred Henry, *Turning Professors into Teachers: A New Approach to Faculty Development and Student Learning* (New York, 1988); Peter Seldin and Associates, *How Administrators Can Improve Teaching: Moving from Talk to Action in Higher Education* (San Francisco, 1990).

For institutions experimenting with collaborative learning, see Karen T. Romer, "Collaboration: New Forms of Learning, New Ways of Thinking," *Forum*, 8 (November/December 1985), 2–18.

CHAPTER 13. DOABLES—CUT COSTS

134 Murray N. Rothbard, "Letter from Academia," *Chronicles*, 15 (September 1991), 48.

134 Henry Beach Needham, "Woodrow Wilson's Views," *Outlook*, 98 (August 26, 1911), 940. (An interview)

For a thoughtful analysis, see Myron Lieberman, "Peer Review and Faculty Self-Government: A Dissenting View," in *Academic Futures: Prospects for Post-Secondary Education*, eds. Waris Shere and Ronald Duhamel (Toronto, Canada, 1987), pp. 79–92.

135 Jonathan Yardley, "The War of Words, From the Trenches," *Washington Post*, January 15, 1990, p. D2.

136 The Western Tradition series was funded by Annenberg/CPB. The two semester course is a sturdy foundation for understanding where we as Americans came from and the relation of the United States to the rest of the world since independence from Great Britain in the eighteenth century.

136 The statistics on lecturing are from Wagner Thielens, Jr., "The Disciplines and Undergraduate Lecturing," p. 7. Paper presented at the annual meetings of the American Educational Research Association, Washington, April 1987. The survey method was random sampling of universities and departments within universities.

137 Lewis J. Perelman, "Closing Education's Technology Gap," *Hudson Institute Briefing Paper*, No. 111, November 28, 1989, p. 6, offers a gloomy report on instructional technology in the public schools, lagging there no doubt for many of the same reasons: "Over 20 years of research shows that computer-assisted instruction, properly employed, can produce at least 30% more learning in 40% less time at 30% less cost than traditional classroom teaching. The cost to the U.S. economy of education's failure to adopt these kinds of proven, on-the-shelf teaching technology on a large scale may be as much as $100 billion a year." The statistics seem inflated, but it's a blockbuster of a statement even if the numbers are reduced by one third.

137 Leslie Spencer, "College Education without the Frills," *Forbes*, 147 (May 27, 1991), 294. Robert J. Samuelson, "School Reform Fraud (Cont'd)," *Newsweek*, 118 (October 28, 1991), 51. See, also, Jack D. Douglas, "Resolving the Crisis in Higher Education," *Cato Policy Report*, 13 (May/June 1991), 1ff.

137 Contact hours or classroom hours are the number of hours per week spent teaching classes. A credit, or credit hour, is generally the same as a contact hour. That is, a three credit course meets for three contact hours per week. Student contact hours are the number of hours per week spent teaching classes multiplied by the number of students in those classes.

138 Robert V. Iosue, "How Colleges Can Cut Costs," *Wall Street Journal*, January 27, 1987, unpaginated.

138 In the second paragraph about Iosue, the quotation is from Robert V. Iosue, "Why Does Tuition Soar? Colleges Get Top-Heavy," *Newsday*, October 2, 1988, p. 4. See also Robert V. Iosue, "Higher Education : Are We Getting Our Money's Worth," in *Leading Pennsylvania into the 21st Century*, ed. Don E. Eberly (Harrisburg, P.A., 1990), pp. 77–96. Iosue retired from the presidency of York College in 1991.

138 The statistic on publications is Ernest L. Boyer, *College: The Undergraduate Experience in America* (New York, 1987), Table 20, p. 129. The exact figures are 48% for research and 51% for doctorate-granting universities. Jay Amberg, "Higher (-Priced) Education," *American Scholar*, 58 (Autumn 1989), 529.

138 Harold E. Yuker, *Faculty Workload: Research, Theory, and Interpretation* (Washington, D.C., 1984), pp. iv, 75, 46, v. See, also, Jon S. Hesseldenz, "Personality-Based Faculty Workload Analysis," *Research in Higher Education*, 5 (1976), 332.

139 Charles J. Sykes, *ProfScam: Professors and the Demise of Higher Education* (New York, 1988), pp. 36–40, reports on the less than savory audit at the University of Wisconsin.

141 The quotation has been attributed to General George Patton, Jr., but a search of the printed sources did not locate it.

141 "Reliable quantitative data are maddeningly absent" is the conclusion of one foundation about the historical evidence relating to faculty teaching loads. (Pew Higher Education Research Program, "The Lattice and the Ratchet," *Policy Perspectives*, 2 (June 1990), 5.) Research universities, now requiring nine hours per week, were more than likely scheduling 15 hours per week fifty years ago in the social sciences and humanities while those now requiring six hours were probably scheduling 12 hours per week fifty years ago. The natural sciences with laboratories should be analyzed separately from the social sciences and humanities, as well as language training within the humanities.

Self-reported statistics for any occupation are suspicious in the absence of congressional legislation punishing transgressors. Stock market investors rest more easily at night knowing there is a Securities and Exchange Commission. Less composed are students of faculty workloads. A careful analyst of university statistics is reduced to word-of-mouth evidence. "Anecdotal reports suggest that the teaching loads of faculty members have been reduced over the past several decades, at least at many research-oriented universities." (Arthur M. Hauptman with Jamie P. Merisotis, *The College Tuition Spiral* (New York, 1990), p. 37.)

Jay Amberg, "Higher (-Priced) Education," *American Scholar,* 58 (Autumn 1989), 521–532, reduces workloads even further: "With sabbaticals and leaves, approximately one-fifth of the professors aren't teaching at all during any given semester." (p. 527).

Hard evidence confirming six hours per week for at least one public university system, State University System of Florida, is Thomas P. Snyder and Eva C. Galambos, *Higher Education Administrative Costs: Continuing the Study* (Washington, 1988), p. 46.

National Center for Education Statistics (U.S. Department of Education), *Profiles of Faculty in Higher Education, 1988* (Washington, D.C., 1991), p. 70, using fall 1987 statistics, puts the number of classroom hours of full-time regular faculty at private research and private doctoral-granting universities at 5.9 and 6.9 and at public research and public doctoral-granting universities at 6.6 and 8.0, respectively.

143 Howard R. Bowen and Jack H. Schuster, *American Professors: A National Resource Imperiled* (New York, 1986), p. 159. The reference refers only to the first quotation in the paragraph citing Bowen and Schuster.

144 Roger L. Geiger, *To Advance Knowledge: The Growth of American Research Universities, 1900–1940* (New York, 1986), pp. 67–77, does the best he can with sparse evidence about the history of teaching loads. The quotation about the egalitarianism of teaching load decision-making is The Pew Higher Education Research Program, "The Lattice and the Ratchet," *Policy Perspectives,* 2 (June 1990), 5–6.

144 The quotation in the Bowen and Schuster paragraph is from Bowen and Schuster, *op. cit.,* pp. 159, 160. The quotation in the following paragraph is from the same source, p. 160.

APPENDIX B. CARNEGIE CLASSIFICATIONS

151 Carnegie Foundation for the Advancement of Teaching, *A Classification of Institutions of Higher Education* (Princeton, NJ, 1987), pp. 7–8, Table 4. The Carnegie Classifications have been consolidated for purposes of clarity. For a more detailed breakdown, see the above reference. It is anticipated that the next report will be published in 1992. The report does not specify whether student enrollment figures are for FTE (full-time equivalency) students or head count. In a telephone conversation (December 18, 1991), the Foundation stated that the figure represents a head count.

APPENDIX C. RANKINGS

153 For the first day's proceedings, see the minutes published by the Association, *Journal of Proceedings and Addresses of the First and Second Annual Conferences*. The initial number of members is greater than twelve because not all originating institutions attended the Chicago meeting in 1900.

NATIONAL SCIENCE FOUNDATION

158 National Science Foundation, *Federal Support to Universities, Colleges, and Nonprofit Institutions: Fiscal Year 1989* (Washington, D.C., 1991), Table B-5, pp. 29–30.

Both Table B-5, presented in the Appendix, and Table C-7 on pp. 136–137, report amounts from the 15 major funding agencies. Table B-5 represents research and development funding in the natural sciences (including engineering) and the social sciences. It excludes funding in the arts and humanities. Table C-7 lists the 100 universities and colleges receiving "the largest amounts" of "federal obligations." Table C-7 includes, in addition to Research and Development, fellowships, plant facilities, funding for the arts and humanities, etc.

The total figure for Table B-5 is $8,516,849,000 and for Table C-7 is $15,657,609,000.

The National Science Foundation states that institutions of higher education "perform about one-half of the Nation's basic research." (p. v) ("Nation's" is in first letter capitals.)

U.S. NEWS TOP 25 NATIONAL UNIVERSITIES

161 "America's Best Colleges," *U.S. News & World Report,* 111 (September 30, 1991), 77–108. Slot number 19 was a tie.

PERSONAL & ACKNOWLEDGEMENTS AND NOTES ON SOURCES

167 Annie Dillard, *The Writing Life* (New York, 1989), p. 44.

168 Shakespeare, *The Tempest,* Act I, Scene 2.

171 Cole Lesley, *Remembered Laughter,* (New York, 1976), p. xx. The words Barrymore used were more earthy but the idea is the same. I am grateful to Arthur Austin of Case Western Reserve University School of Law for tracing the source of this quotation.

INDEX

ABOUT THE AUTHOR

Richard M. Huber is a recognized scholar and teacher. He holds a B.A. from Princeton and a Ph.D. in American Studies from Yale. Academically, Dr. Huber has taught at Princeton and served for many years as a dean at Hunter College in New York. He has achieved numerous honors, awards, and fellowships for scholarship and writing.

In other areas, Dr. Huber has moderated several television series on public affairs and has authored the widely acclaimed *The American Idea of Success*, considered to be the standard work on the subject. Currently, he is conducting workshops at the U.S. State Department for foreign service officers headed overseas.